Implementing Electronic Document and Record Management Systems

Implementing Electronic Document and Record Management Systems

Azad Adam

Auerbach Publications
Taylor & Francis Group
Boca Raton   New York

Auerbach Publications is an imprint of the
Taylor & Francis Group, an **informa** business

Auerbach Publications
Taylor & Francis Group
6000 Broken Sound Parkway NW, Suite 300
Boca Raton, FL 33487-2742

© 2008 by Taylor & Francis Group, LLC
Auerbach is an imprint of Taylor & Francis Group, an Informa business

Library of Congress Cataloging-in-Publication Data

Adam, Azad.
    Implementing electronic document and record management systems / Azad Adam.
        p. cm.
    Includes bibliographical references and index.
    ISBN 978-0-8493-8059-4 (alk. paper)
    1. Electronic filing systems. 2. Business records--Data processing--Management. 3. Public records--Data processing--Management. 4. Medical records--Data processing--Management. 5. Records--Management--Data processing. 6. Electronic records--Management. 7. Text processing (Computer science) I. Title.

HF5738.A32 2007
651.5'9--dc22   2007013892

Visit the Taylor & Francis Web site at
http://www.taylorandfrancis.com

and the Auerbach Web site at
http://www.auerbach-publications.com

Dedication

For Humza, Medina, and Yusuf, may their futures be bright
and filled with opportunities!

To Mum, Dad, Isaac, and Tariq for helping and supporting me
through all the ups and downs!

To Olive, for helping me to realise my potential
and for helping me go for it!

To Andrew, for being there, for standing firm,
and for all the support you have given me!

A special thanks to Vickie Hewson for all your help, support,
and determination on the project!

Contents

Part 2   Components of EDRMS

Part 3   A Framework for EDRMS

Part 4   EDRMS Case Studies

Preface

Why write a book about implementing electronic document and records management systems (EDRMS)?

Well, back in early 2003 I was working for a local government organization in southeast England and was given the task of implementing an electronic document and records management system as part of the Implementing Electronic Government (IEG) program, and it soon became apparent that nobody had actually implemented a full blown EDRMS solution across a whole public sector organization, such as local council offices. Hence, implementing EDRMS became a project of being chucked in at the deep end, and also a project of trial and error.

The project lasted for over two and a half years by which time I had realized that I had gained quite significant experience in implementing EDRMS, especially within local council environments, and the initial thoughts regarding writing a book about the topic came to mind.

In January 2006 I decided to take the plunge and prepare a book proposal. To my delight it was accepted, and I then began the long task of writing down my experiences.

During my time working for the local government organization, as we implemented their EDRMS solution it dawned upon us just how important the aspects of cultural change are on an organization with regard to the impact a system like EDRMS can have.

To sum this up, the technical implementation of EDRMS was the easy part. What presented the challenge was getting the organization and the users in the organization to accept the new system and to let go of working with paper files and folders.

As well as the importance of managing the cultural change associated with implementing EDRMS, the need for strong project management throughout every single phase of the project also became apparent.

Implementing EDRMS is not just about technology—that's the easy part! It's more about people, organizations, organizational culture, change, cultural change, managing cultural change, and good, strong, yet flexible project management.

The book also explores reasons for implementing EDRMS—essentially answering the question, why implement an EDRMS solution?—and presents the reader with compelling arguments to justify the implementation of such a system across a broad range of organizations, discussing the benefits to be achieved, the costs that can be reduced, and productivity gains that can be achieved.

It has been my aim to make this book as practical as possible and, as such, I have included steps that can be followed in determining the specification for the basic component parts of an organization's EDRMS solution, as well as discussing how to produce key documents such as the business case, feasibility study, functional requirements, and technical requirements. Short descriptions of the EDRMS software offerings are also presented in Appendix A of this book.

In writing this book I have aimed to present the reader with the mix of theory, technology, change management and project management, and key documents required for successful implementation of EDRMS.

Acknowledgments

Writing a book just doesn't happen in isolation. It takes a collaborative effort from many people. First and foremost, I would like to acknowledge my family and friends for believing in me and supporting me throughout the writing of this book. I would like to thank John Wyzaleck, acquisitions editor at Auerbach, for believing in my proposal and giving me the opportunity to make this book happen, and for supporting me and encouraging me with my writing. A thank you to Catherine Giacari, my project coordinator, for all your help, and to Gerry Jaffe, my project editor, for your assistance in turning the manuscript into this book.

Introduction

In recent years there has been a worldwide shift toward electronic government and delivering citizen services online, using the Internet, one-stop shops, centralized call centers, etc., without the need for people to be physically present at offices. This in turn means that public sector organizations need to be able to access information quickly, easily, and efficiently. The vast majority of public sector organizations worldwide have used paper files and folders for hundreds of years, and hence this has become part of their ingrained culture.

With the emphasis now on delivering citizen services online using modern communications methods such as the Internet and mobile phone-based services, this gives rise to the need for electronic document and records storage in order to quickly and efficiently access whatever information is needed by the citizen (client) in order to deliver the services required.

The vast majority of public sector organizations have not implemented any form of electronic and document records management system (EDRMS) across the whole of their organization. The nearest most have come is in implementing systems within particular key sections, such as social services and welfare. Hence, records and information are often duplicated, and there is no one central source of information. A properly structured and implemented EDRM system would address this need, offering quick and easy access to documents and records and serving the whole organization from this one central data source.

In the U.K., the implementation of EDRMS by 2004 was a priority outcome of Implementing Electronic Government (IEG) as outlined by the Office of the Deputy Prime Minister (ODPM), as well as the Freedom of Information Act (FOIA). However, the challenge that faces many heads of ICT (information and communications technology), project managers, and business analysts is they find it quite a daunting prospect to implement

EDRMS, which is essentially a computer system that will contain electronic copies of an organization's paper-based documents and records. Another added complication is managing the cultural change and subsequent business process reengineering within the organization involved in the change from using paper-based documents and records to using electronic documents and records that can be routed across the organization.

This book, *Implementing Electronic Document and Records Management Systems*, will provide readers, whether they are IT managers, project managers, or business analysts, with direction and guidance in implementing EDRMS within their organization. This book draws heavily from the real life experiences of the author who has implemented electronic document and records management systems in a number of public sector organizations in the U.K.

Foremost, *Implementing Electronic Document and Records Management Systems* discusses the reasons why organizations of all sizes across all sectors need to move away from working with paper-based records and move toward implementing an EDRMS, in terms of complying with new legislation and the FOIA (Freedom of Information Act). Increased efficiency and productivity issues regarding the successful implementation of EDRMS are also discussed.

Providing the reader with a step-by-step guide to implementing a successful system, this book is divided into four parts:

Part 1, "Basics of EDRMS," presents the reader with a solid understanding of EDRMS, starting off with the history and then moving on to discuss the fundamentals aspects, and finally discussing the necessary issues of complying with both standards and legislation.

Part 2, "Components of EDRMS," contains eight chapters and discusses the major individual component parts that make up an EDRM system, covering areas such as creating electronic document types, creating the folder structure, e-mail management, search and retrieval, integrating workflow, user interfaces, mobile working, and remote access. Finally the topic of scanning historical documents and records is covered along with two case studies illustrating how organizations have converted paper to electronic images.

Part 3, "A Framework for EDRMS," runs through the specific steps needed to complete an EDRMS implementation from the first concept idea through to implementation and ongoing support for the project. Project management is discussed in detail with the PRINCE2 and PMBOK methodologies explored. This part of the book also covers the critical documents that are needed for EDRMS implementation such as the Business Case, Functional Requirements, and Technical Requirements. EDRMS software platforms are explored in Chapter 18, along with hardware considerations in Chapter 19. Chapter 20 then discusses the need to manage the cultural change created by EDRMS, and discusses approaches in change management and implementing a change program. Finally, Chapter 21 concludes this section of the book by discussing the ongoing nature of the project.

Part 4 presents the reader with a number of case studies that examine how various organizations across the globe have implemented EDRM systems. Appendix A contains listings of EDRMS software vendors with short descriptions of their product offerings, and Appendix B contains a glossary.

To get the most from this book and any possible EDRMS implementation, it is recommended that you read it in its entirety first before working with the processes and procedures discussed.

About the Author

Azad Adam is a freelance IT consultant specializing in the area of electronic document and records management systems, mainly working within U.K. public sector organizations where he undertakes systems design and implementation projects connected with EDRMS solutions.

Azad started his career in IT in the 1990s, at a relatively young age, by first offering computer support services to small business owners in London. From there, he progressed to working as a freelance IT contractor specializing in Web development and Web content management solutions, and has worked as a senior Web developer across a variety of organizations from wide-ranging sectors such as charity, retail and investment banking, new media companies, and government organizations.

Azad can be contacted at azadadam@hotmail.com.

Part 1

BASICS OF ELECTRONIC DOCUMENT AND RECORDS MANAGEMENT SYSTEMS

Chapter 1

History and Background of Electronic Document and Records Management Systems

Earliest Systems Known to Humans

The task of managing documents and records goes far back, even before the beginning of civilization. Our early ancestors, the cavemen, used to draw pictures on the walls of their caves, depicting events of their times. This can be thought of as the earliest known form of record keeping, i.e., recording events for future reference. Egyptian hieroglyphics are another example of primitive record keeping. In both these cases, historians have been able to obtain information indirectly about the environment and activities of people from bygone eras.

Modern Systems

Let us fast-forward to modern times: In the 1980s, most of the systems available were Document Image Processing (DIP) systems, essentially the electronic equivalent of a filing cabinet, with the facility for documents to be scanned, indexed, and stored in the system, so they could later be retrieved for viewing on screen or printing.

Some of the more advanced DIP systems also included elements of workflow, which allowed the organization to route scanned documents (images) around the organization. For example, an organization could scan their incoming mail, and then those scanned images could be routed to designated staff to process. Electronic Document Management Systems (EDMS) as well as Electronic Records Management Systems (ERMS) emerged in the 1990s.

EDMS generally integrated with applications such as Microsoft Office and allowed users to actively manage documents, which could be stored and indexed in a document repository. They could be checked in and checked out and versions and revision cycles tracked using versioning control. Some of these systems also included DIP functionality, which allowed both conventional paper and electronic files to be scanned, indexed, and archived.

ERMS first started appearing in the 1990s. These systems mainly managed the physical location of paper-based records, essentially an electronic index for paper files and folders. Gradually, these systems developed into systems for managing electronic records and electronic documents, providing DIP and workflow functionality, as well. However, these new hybrid systems of records, documents, imaging, and workflow were relatively new and immature without any definite standards for record-keeping compliance.

During the mid-to-late 1990s, standards for ERMS started to be developed. In the United Kingdom, the Public Records Office (PRO), which is now The National Archives (TNA), initiated a project with central government to develop a set of functional requirements for electronic record-keeping systems. The first version of these requirements was published in 1999. In 2002, TNA issued a new version of the functional requirements document for ERMS with more detailed information regarding metadata standards, developed as part of the e-government program of the United Kingdom.

In the United States, the Department of Defense (DoD) 5015.2-STD, "Design Criteria Standards for Electronic Records Management Software Applications," was first released in late 1997. The standard was developed by the DoD, updated, and reissued on June 19, 2002. The standard sets forth mandatory functional requirements for ERMS software, as well as guidelines for the management of classified records. DoD 5015.2 is currently the de facto standard in the United States.

In 2001, the International Organization for Standardization (ISO) released its standard for records management, ISO 15489, based on the Australian standard AS 4390-1996. Later, the Australian government withdrew AS 4390-1996 and replaced it with ISO 15489. In addition to the

ISO standard, a European standard known as MOREQ, developed by the IDABC (Interoperable Delivery of European eGovernment Services to public Administrations, Businesses, and Citizens), has also been released.

So from virtually no standards back in the mid-1990s, there are now a number of standards relating to records management. Those most in use are the TNA 2002 in the United Kingdom and DoD 5015.2 in the United States. Both TNA 2002 and DoD 5015.2 define the functional requirements for ERMS. Most of the major EDRM vendors comply with at least one of these standards, if not both.

Future Market Trends

Currently, there are mature standards for records management and no shortage of software vendors offering document and records management system solutions, so where is the market going?

There is no doubt that nearly all the software vendors offering combined electronic document and records management solutions, as well as separate document and records management solutions provide these as part of a bigger Enterprise Content Management solution.

Enterprise Content Management is a framework of applications, including content management, document management, records management, Web content management, scanning and imaging tools, and collaboration tools, as well as workflow and business process reengineering tools. Enterprise Content Management solutions are normally aimed at larger organizations.

Chapter 2

Fundamentals of EDRMS

This chapter presents an overview of the fundamental aspects of different kinds of document and record management systems and technologies, starting off with a discussion of legislation concerning records and information. The chapter then discusses fundamental components of systems, as well as presenting and explaining commonly used acronyms currently in use.

Legislative Issues

Whenever any organization of any size retains information, especially when this relates to individuals, there are certain legal requirements that need to be followed regarding the recording of documents and records.

It is beyond the scope of this book to cover all the legalities of storing information relating to individuals using electronic methods. Some important legislation need to be referred to within the United States, such as the Privacy Act 1974 and the Freedom of Information Act. In the United Kingdom the Data Protection Act 1998 as well as the Freedom of Information Act 2000 need to be adhered to.

Legislation — Freedom of Information Act, Privacy Act 1974, Data Protection Act 1998

The Freedom of Information Act is particularly important. Broadly speaking, under this legislation, citizens have a right to request almost any type of information from any organization within a specific time period. Needless to say, it greatly helps an organization to have an adequate document and record-keeping system in place to comply with freedom of information requests. Freedom of information laws exist both in the United States and United Kingdom.

The Privacy Act 1974 is a U.S. Act concerned with how information relating to citizens is stored and what rights they have regarding access to the information stored about themselves.

The Data Protection Act 1998 is broadly speaking, the UK equivalent of the Privacy Act 1974 in the United States. It is concerned with how personal information relating to individuals is processed and handled.

The Freedom of Information Act, the Privacy Act, and the Data Protection Act, among other acts of Law will be covered in greater detail in Chapter 3, "Complying with Standards and Legislation."

The Difference between Documents and Records

The Oxford English Dictionary defines the word document as "a piece of written, printed, or electronic matter that provides information or evidence." The word record is defined as "a piece of evidence or information constituting an account of something that has occurred, been said, etc." In electronic document and records management systems (EDRMS), a record can be defined as an electronic folder consisting of one or more documents.

From the preceding definitions, where documents, that is, "written, printed, or electronic matter that provides information or evidence," are contained in a folder all of which relate to a specific matter, or give the account over time of a specific matter, this would effectively create a record, which is "a piece of evidence or information constituting an account of something that has occurred, been said, etc."

Consider for example, a planning or building application made to a council or municipality office. A person or organization submits a set of documents, which may include an application form, and the architect's drawings and reports. These documents would then be placed in a new folder, i.e., a record, either electronic or manual, would be created to contain these documents. As the application progresses through various stages, the record concerning that particular planning application would have other documents placed in it. Thus we have on file (electronic or otherwise) all documents that make up the record of what has happened with that particular planning application.

Another crucial difference between documents and records is that documents can change, whereas records do not and must not, change. A record is a document or set of documents, all relating to a specific matter that has happened in the past. So, it is a record of history. As with the planning application, whenever documents are placed in the file, they become records if those documents are not subject to change. For example, the documents that make up the planning application would become a record of the planning application procedure.

A document, on the other hand, is something that could be a work in progress, which is subject to change and therefore not a record. Documents can and do become records once they are set in stone, so to speak, and do not undergo changes, i.e., once those documents describe an event that has happened in the past, whether 2 minutes or 20 years ago.

Acronyms

The computer software that enables a computer system to store documents and records in an electronic format is referred to by many different names and acronyms. A list of commonly used acronyms is provided in Figure 2.1.

EDRMS — Electronic Document and Records Management Systems

EDRMS refer to systems that are capable of handling both electronic documents and records.

Acronym	Actual Words
EDRMS	Electronic Document and Records Management System
EDMS	Electronic Document Management System
EDM	Electronic Document Management
ERM	Electronic Records Management
ERMS	Electronic Records Management System
DMS	Document Management System
DIP	Digital Image Processing
ECM	Enterprise Content Management
RM	Records Management
DM	Document Management

Figure 2.1   List of commonly used acronyms.

EDRM — Electronic Document and Records Management

This is essentially the same as EDRMS but without the word system. In some places this book uses the acronym EDRMS whereas in others it refers to EDRM followed by the word system, i.e., "EDRM system" as opposed to "EDRMS." There is essentially no difference between these two acronyms, and the reason for their alternate use is only semantic — for more flowing sentences and discussions.

EDMS — Electronic Document Management Systems

EDMS mainly refer to systems that are designed primarily to deal with electronic document management.

EDM — Electronic Document Management

This is the same as EDMS but without the word system, similar to EDRM mentioned previously. The same holds true for EDMS and EDM.

ERMS — Electronic Records Management Systems

ERMS refers to systems that are designed for electronic record keeping, archiving, and storage. Many of these systems also have integrated document management capabilities.

ERM — Electronic Records Management

This acronym is the same as ERMS but without the word system. As previously mentioned under EDRM, both "ERMS" and "ERM system" are the same in this text, and the acronyms are used as appropriate, for better sentence construction.

DMS — Document Management Systems

DMS refers to systems that have been designed to manage documents. The absence of the word "electronic" would indicate that DMS is a system that is capable of managing both electronic and manual documents. However, 99 times out of 100, DMS would nowadays refer to an electronic system.

ECM — Enterprise Content Management

ECM commonly refers to suites of applications, normally from one particular vendor, that are designed for content management, document management, records management, collaboration services, and workflow and Web content management as their main primary activities. An ECM system is one that has been developed and designed to manage all content, whether it be documents or records, or whatever else that constitutes content within an organization.

DM and RM

Other commonly used terms are DM for document management and RM for record management. Some vendors use these terms to describe their products, e.g., ACME DM or ACME RM. In other cases, these terms will simply be used as abbreviations as already mentioned.

Electronic Record Keeping

At times the text in this book will also refer to electronic record keeping or electronic records-keeping systems. These terms are employed in place of ERM and ERMS in Chapter 3, because the standards discussed in that chapter use these terms, and not ERM or ERMS. However, they refer to the same system, and no difference between them should be inferred.

Basic Components of Electronic Document Management Systems

The basic components of an EDMS are listed in Figure 2.2. With almost all commercially available EDM systems, there will be functionality that will cross over into the areas of workflow, collaboration, record management, and archiving and imaging. This happens because software vendors tend to target their products at particular target audiences and will often incorporate other functionality that is needed alongside core EDMS functionality.

Document Repository

All EDM systems need to have a document repository. This is where the system stores documents that are under its management. Most commonly,

Document Repository
Integration with Desktop Applications
Check-In and Check-Out
Versioning
Auditing
Security
Classification and Indexing
Search and Retrieval

Figure 2.2   Basic components of electronic document management systems.

the document repository will be on the hard disk of a networked server. The document repository could be in just one location on one particular server or could be distributed across many different servers. Hence, the repository should be a central store for all the documents in the organization, allowing users to retrieve them from the repository via the search and retrieval or browsing functionality.

The core idea of having a document repository could fail if users in the organization do not place documents in the repository when they are created. However, a properly implemented EDM system would ensure that documents are placed in the repository on creation. This could be achieved if users are allowed to save documents to the repository only and, possibly, not permitted to save documents to their local hard drives or other network locations, these features being disabled at the desktop application level. For example, the Save functionality in a word processor, spreadsheet, or any other desktop application software could be configured to allow saving to the EDMS document repository only, which leads to another area of functionality known as Integration with Desktop Applications.

Besides an EDM system having a document repository, the system would also use a database of some kind to store information about the documents. This is often referred to as metadata, and will be covered in greater depth later in this section.

Folder Structures

The EDM system should allow a system administrator to set up and maintain an organized folder structure allowing for documents and files to be placed within folders according to their classification. The folder structure could be set up to follow the organizational structure, or it could be project based, representing projects within the organization, or business function based or property based. The folder structure could also be set up in a combination of the organizational structure and project-based structure, or it could be a combination of business function and property-based structure. Whichever is decided upon, the EDM system should allow a system administrator to set up and maintain a folder structure.

Integration with Desktop Applications

An EDM system needs to integrate with desktop applications, thereby allowing users to save documents straight from the application the document was created in, as mentioned in the preceding section on the document repository. The vast majority of EDM systems integrate with many popular desktop application suites such as Microsoft Office.

Check-In and Check-Out

Check-in and Check-out is a feature of EDM systems that controls who is editing a document and when it is being edited, and also ensures that not more than one person edits a document at any one time. For example, if a user needs to edit a document, it is checked out to that particular user who is thereby allowed to edit the document; other users in the organization would only be able view that document but not edit it, i.e., the document is in read-only mode to everybody else except the person who has checked out the document and is editing it. When the user who has checked out the document has finished editing it, he or she can then check in the document, thereby saving the updated copy to the document repository, allowing other users to access the updated document. After a document has been updated, the system needs to keep track of the changes. This is accomplished by versioning and auditing.

Version Control

After a document has been updated, there needs to be a mechanism by which the system can keep track of the changes made to that document. This is achieved by assigning the document a version number. For example, when a document is created and first saved into the document repository, it will be assigned a version number of 1.0. After it has been updated, the document could be assigned a version number of 1.1. The next time it is updated, it may be assigned the version number 1.2, and so on. With major revisions of the document, the version number can increase by one whole increment; for example, the document version could go from 1.2 to 2.0. Besides keeping track of version numbers, the system should allow authorized users access to previous versions of the document.

Auditing

Auditing, along with version control, keeps a check on which users made changes to a document and when. The auditing feature would allow authorized users to find out the changes that have been made to the document since it was first created. For example, if a document is currently in version 1.3, then the auditing feature would allow authorized users to run a report to enable them to find out when the document was first created, the date it was updated and by which user, and what were the exact changes that were made to the document when it was updated.

To sum up, auditing allows you to discover the changes that were made, when they were made, and who made them.

Security

Security is an extremely important component in a properly implemented system. Security should be tightly integrated with the system, allowing for security access permissions to be applied at different levels within the system. For example, the system should allow an administrator to apply specific security settings to an individual document, thereby specifying that certain users or a certain group of users can both read and make changes to a certain document, whereas other users may only be able to read that document but not make any changes; still other users may not even be able to see that particular document.

An administrator of a system or a certain section of the system should also be able to set up and maintain security settings on individual files, folders, or groups of folders within the system, again allowing for read, write, or no access security permissions to be set up, as necessary.

Classification and Indexing

All documents should be classified and indexed using metadata, thereby allowing them to be easily retrieved at a later date using a search mechanism. The metadata should contain information about the document, such as the author, the document title, the date it was created, the subject of the document, and the department where the document originates, among other information. If a document is properly classified and indexed, then it can be easily found using search and retrieval mechanisms by users within the organization.

Search and Retrieval

Searching and retrieving documents is the other half of classifying and indexing documents. When documents are classified and indexed, they are placed into the EDMS document repository in a systematically organized fashion. The more intuitive the classification and indexing of documents is, the easier it will be to locate them using the search and retrieval mechanism.

A good system should offer users multiple ways in which to locate (search and retrieve) documents using a few different mechanisms, such as browsing the folder structure, a basic search, and an advanced search.

A basic search should simply allow the user to type in keywords and then retrieve all documents in which the keywords match either the metadata or the document's content. An advanced search should allow the user to search individual metadata fields, allowing them to combine the metadata fields into the search criteria, so that either all metadata field values match (known as an AND statement) or either one of the metadata fields match (known as an OR statement). The advanced search should also allow the user to combine metadata search criteria as well as search for words or phrases within the document content. For example, consider the document described in Figure 2.2. Using an advanced search, the user may want to locate all documents written by the author "Azad Adam" that contain the phrase "night sky" in the document content. The user would specify "Azad Adam" in the author search field and also the phrase "night sky" in the document content search field. The search would then return this document and all other documents that match the search criteria in the search results.

The EDM system should also offer users the ability to browse for documents by manually going through the folder structure, just as they would browse for documents using Windows Explorer.

Optical Character Recognition (OCR)

OCR is a method used to index the typed content of documents, which then allows the typed content to be searched upon. For example, again let us consider the following short document as illustrated in (Figure 2.3). If the document's content has not been indexed using OCR, then users searching for this document would only be able to search for it based on

Title	Short collection of Phrases
Author	Azad Adam
Subject	Phrases of the English Language
Creation Date	25/05/2006
Document Content	The quick brown fox jumps over the fence and away from the lazy dog. The cat sat on the mat. The moon in the night sky is very bright. The sun sets over London City.

Figure 2.3 Example document used for OCR.

the Title, Author or Subject fields, meaning they would have to know either some or all of the document's title or the document's subject, or the name of the author of the document in order to locate it.

If the document content has been indexed using OCR, then the content of the document would also be searchable, meaning that a user could locate the document simply by typing in the words "lazy dog" or "London" or "cat."

Indexing the document's content is a very powerful feature because users may know that they want to locate a document about a "lazy dog," for instance, but may not know the document's title, subject, or the author's name.

Basic Components of Record Management Systems

The vast majority of ERMS are either used in conjunction with EDMS or contain document management functionality even though there may not be a mention of the word document in the product description. An ERMS will share some common functionality with an EDMS.

Repository

As with EDM systems, all ERM systems will need to have a repository where the records are archived. Physically, the repository will be located on one or more networked database servers but will appear to users of the system as one central repository. Users of the ERM system should have the ability to browse the repository if their user access rights allow them to do so.

Folder Structure

The folder structure of an ERM system will exist within the repository and allows the system administrators to systematically categorize where records are archived within the system. Using a hierarchical folder structure will allow the administrator to set it up to either represent the organizational structure, business function-based structure, project-based structure, or property-based structure, or represent a combination of all four structures to facilitate the archival of records.

Classification, Indexing, and Metadata

All records in the system need to be categorized and indexed within the folder structure, using metadata to archive records in a systematic manner, and to help users to find their documents in the future using the search and retrieval mechanisms.

Capturing and Declaring Records

An ERM system needs a method automatically capturing and declaring records. For example, take an organization that processes forms and sends out acknowledgment letters to clients. Once they receive and process the client's form, it will become a record of the interaction with the client. The subsequent acknowledgment letter they send out will be another document that also becomes a part of the record of the interaction with that particular client.

Hence, if the system did not automatically capture and declare these documents as records, they would either not get declared as records, or it would be left to a user in the organization to manually declare those documents as records, in which case human error can and will creep into the process, resulting in their not being properly archived as records.

Retention and Disposal of Records

ERM systems need to be able to retain records for a specific length of time, depending on the nature of the records, and also dispose of them when that time limit is up. Consider a banking institution that offers members of the general public bank accounts. When customers close their accounts with the bank, the bank will be obliged to keep details of their accounts on record for a set period of time. Let us say the period for keeping accounts on record after they are closed is seven years. Then, from the date of account closure, the system should automatically keep all the details relating to the customers and their accounts on record until seven years in the future. Once the time has expired, seven years in this case, the system should dispose of the records, either completely deleting them securely from the system or moving them to off-line storage, depending on organizational rules.

Record Security

ERM systems need to employ stringent security around the archiving of records, both for the organization's own security and to comply with legislation such as the Data Protection Act and the Privacy Act. Electronic records should be secured in such a way that only authorized users within the organization have access to them. Administrators of the ERM system should be able to easily set up and maintain record security within the system.

Managing Physical Records

An ERM should be capable of not only managing electronic records but also physical records existing in physical locations such as filing rooms and filing cabinets.

The system should be able to provide authorized users with details of where they can locate physical records and should also provide functionality for users to note on the system if they have removed records from their physical location — essentially, a type of check-out procedure for physical records stored on the system.

Search and Retrieval

As mentioned previously in the section on search and retrieval functionality regarding EDM systems, an ERM system needs to have the same search and retrieval functionality of a basic and advanced search, as well as the ability for users to browse the repository. Additionally, the search mechanism needs to be able to search across electronic records and physical records, if any, managed by the system.

A combined EDRM system should allow the use of one search mechanism, either basic or advanced, to search both documents and records and, when performing searches, should not distinguish between documents in progress or archived records. This is particularly important because if a user has a need to find information on a certain client, then there may be a number of documents that currently represent work in progress and a number of them that have become historic records. All of this information will be of importance to the user who will probably not know the differences between documents and records. Hence, the mechanism needs to be able to search across both documents and records, and this fact should be transparent to the user.

Auditing and Reporting

Auditing and reporting is an important feature of both records management and document management, and the system should provide functionality to allow authorized users and administrators facilities to produce audit trails concerning records and documents in terms of access and changes, dates created, dates modified, etc. Reporting facilities should be flexible enough to allow users to create bespoke reports regarding documents or records.

Compliance with Standards

Legislation such as the Freedom of Information Act, the Privacy Act, and the Data Protection Act, as well as standards such as DoD 5015.2, TNA 2002, ISO 15489, and MOREQ, are key drivers of the development of EDRM systems. Therefore, for systems to be compliant and legally accountable, both document and record management systems need to follow the relative legislation and standards that apply to both the organization and the country in which they are being implemented. Most systems from major electronic documents and records software vendors comply with one or more of these standards.

Scanning and Imaging

Facilities to scan and image paper-based documents need to be part of an ERM system because one of the main business drivers for organizations implementing these systems is the need to provide staff with instant access to centrally held information and free up space used for filing rooms.

Some ERM and EDRM systems have integrated scanning and imaging modules allowing the organization to scan documents in batches and index them, whereas other software vendors provide scanning and imaging functionality as an optional module.

Collaboration

Collaborative services allow people and teams within the organization to communicate and share information, for example, to work on documents together. Although collaborative services are not a mandatory requirement of an EDRM system, it is certainly a very useful feature to have integrated with the system. Hence, if an EDRM system's task is to manage documents and records, then it makes sense to include functionality to encourage staff in the organization to share information and work together when necessary on relevant documents and records.

Workflow

Workflow, also referred to as business process management (BPM), is used to manage the flow of information around an organization. For example, take an invoicing system; an invoice is received through the post, gets scanned on to the system, then gets routed to accounts, may then have to go to a particular person within the accounts department for authorization, and then goes into a queue to be paid via a check run. The steps involved in the invoice being electronically routed around an organization from one person to the next is called Workflow.

As with collaboration mentioned previously workflow is not strictly within the ambit of EDRM systems, but it is an extremely useful feature that, when properly implemented, can speed up processes, making them more efficient, eliminating the paper trail while providing accountability for each task assigned to an individual. Chapter 7 covers workflow and business process reengineering in greater depth.

The Complete EDRMS

The exact functionality required of an EDRM system will differ from organization to organization, depending on their specific needs and objectives. There is, however, a core set of functionality that an EDRM system should provide. This is document management, records management, scanning and imaging, as well as some collaboration and workflow functionality.

Some vendors offer a modular approach to EDRMS, offering separate document management, records management, scanning and imaging, workflow, and collaboration software products, allowing a system to be built up as needs and requirements change and also allowing an organization to purchase just the modules relevant to their needs.

Other vendors offer products that may include both document management and collaboration as one product and then offer document and records management functionality in another product. The vast majority of vendors will have optional modules allowing a system to be tailored to an organization's unique needs and requirements.

Whichever type of system is decided upon, it would make sense to implement one that has the capability to be scaled up both in terms of size and functionality. For example, an organization may want to implement just document management and collaboration to start with, and then, the following year, implement record management and workflow.

Chapter 3

Complying with Standards and Legislation

Before actually implementing EDRMS, it is important to comply with the standards used for the storage and retrieval of electronic documents and records. Complying with standards helps organizations stay within the laws and regulations of the country they are operating in regarding the retention of information.

Although complying with standards can help organizations stay within laws and regulations, it should not be seen as a foolproof method of complying with any particular country's laws and regulations concerning the retention of information, especially relating to private information held by individual citizens.

Organizations and individuals charged with implementing systems to retain information are therefore advised to seek legal clarification from legal counsel in their respective countries before implementing such a system.

Three of the most common and well-known standards currently in use are ISO 15489, an international standard, MOREQ, a European standard, DoD 5015.2 in the U.S., and AS ISO 15489 in Australia.

In discussing ISO 15489, the terms records management and records keeping have been used in place of EDRMS. The two terms have been used because ISO 15489 is a standard concerned with both paper and electronic documents and records and their associated information management systems.

ISO 15489

ISO 15489 is an international standard that defines best practices for the management of both paper and electronic documents and records. The ISO 15489 standard is defined and maintained by the International Organization for Standardization, or ISO for short. It is based on the Australian standard AS 4390-1996: Records Management, which has promoted best practice for records keeping. After the ISO released ISO 15489, the Australian government withdrew the Australian standard AS 4390-1996, replacing it with AS ISO 15489.

The ISO 15489 standard is aimed at all organizations who need to ensure that their documents and records are properly maintained, accessible, categorized, and indexed from the start of the documents' or records' life, which would be their creation, to the end of their life, which could be either the disposal, archiving, or moving of the documents or records to off-line/off-site storage.

Disposing of documents or records at the end of their life should be carried out according to predetermined rules, detailed in Chapter 9, "Records Management and Record Management Policies," as retention guidelines and also throughout the rest of this book.

The standard is divided into two parts; *ISO 15489.1-2002, Records Management — Part 1: General* and *ISO 15489.2-2002, Records Management — Part 2: Guidelines.*

ISO 15489.1-2002, Records Management — Part 1: General

Part 1 provides a high-level framework for record keeping and discusses high-level records management requirements and the design of a records management system. In particular, the benefits to the organization of records management are discussed, as well the complying with legislation and the need to assign and assume responsibility for adequate records management policies and procedures.

The processes of records management are also laid out in Part 1, and these cover records capture, such as imaging and uploading documents into the system, and storing and retaining records in the system, the latter known as the retention of records. Retrieving and accessing documents and records is discussed, as well as auditing records and the need to keep audit trails. Part 1 also discusses the need for training and support for all users in the organization. These processes have been developed into a methodology known as DIRKS (Designing and Implementing Record Keeping Systems).

ISO 15489.2-2002, Records Management — Part 2: Guidelines

Part 2 is a technical report that provides practical guidance on how to implement an effective records management system as described in Part 1 using the DIRKS methodology. Practical guidance is given on the records management functions of capturing, classifying, storing, accessing, and managing records, as well as on the security of documents and records, and developing a classification scheme.

Guidance is also given on establishing monitoring, auditing, and training programs as part of the records management system implementation and ongoing use within the organization.

Complying with ISO 15489 can help to reassure customers and clients of the organization that documents and records are held and maintained according to a stated policy and an international standard. The ISO 15489 standard can be accessed online at www.iso.org.

DIRKS (Designing and Implementing Record-Keeping Systems)

DIRKS is an eight-step methodology designed for helping organizations implement effective record-keeping systems, first developed by Archives Authority of New South Wales as part of their Electronic Recordkeeping Project shortly after the release of the Australian standard AS 4390-1996, Records Management. The DIRKS methodology is included in ISO 15489, the international standard, and AS ISO 15489, the Australian standard.

The eight steps of the DIRKS methodology are listed in Figure 3.1. The DIRKS methodology has been designed to be very flexible, allowing an organization to implement it in a nonlinear way. For example, you could start with Step B: Analysis of Business Activity and then move on to Step C: Identification of Recordkeeping Requirements, and then jump to Step F: Design of Recordkeeping Systems. You can also work through some of the steps concurrently, running certain processes in parallel with others. For example, you may complete some parts of Step C: Identification of Recordkeeping Requirements research during the course of your work on Step A: Preliminary Investigation, and Step B: Analysis of Business Activity.

Step A — Preliminary Investigation

Preliminary investigation is concerned with collecting information to identify the organization's legislative requirements regarding record keeping

Step A	Preliminary investigation
Step B	Analysis of business activity
Step C	Identification of recordkeeping requirements
Step D	Assessment of existing systems
Step E	Identification of strategies for recordkeeping
Step F	Design of a recordkeeping system
Step G	Implementation of a recordkeeping system
Step H	Post implementation review

Figure 3.1   Steps in the DIRKS methodology.

and to gage an understanding of the organization's needs as to why they create and maintain records. An awareness of the organization's business activities, technology infrastructure, and record-keeping risks are also required during this step. This step is essentially a fact-finding exercise.

Step B — Analysis of Business Activity

Analysis of business activity is concerned with identifying and documenting the organization's business functions, activities, and transactions, and determining how and when these are performed, where they are performed, and by whom and in what capacity. This step is essentially the who, why, where, when, and how of the organization's business processes.

Step C — Identification of Record-Keeping Requirements

The identification of record-keeping requirements step requires the examination of all legal and business activities as well as any other sources of interaction within the organization in order to determine the requirements for evidence and information concerning documents and records in regard to record-keeping for the organization.

Step D — Assessment of Existing Systems

This step requires the assessment of existing systems used to perform business operations and processes within the organization in order to determine its record-keeping needs and also identify where these systems do not require enhanced record-keeping requirements.

Step E — Identification of Strategies for Record-Keeping

This step is used to determine the requirements needed to enable systems to meet record-keeping requirements and choose and determine strategies that fit into the needs and culture of the organization.

Step F — Design of a Record-Keeping System

This step is used to design a record-keeping system that meets the strategies determined in Step E — identification of strategies for record keeping.

Step G — Implementation of a Record-Keeping System

This step ensures that all components of the new or redesigned systems meet the organization's requirements. It is also used to implement a training program for users of the system as well as to roll out the system and manage the change within the organization.

Step H — Post-Implementation Review

This step is used for gathering information on the effectiveness of the new record-keeping systems as well user feedback while rectifying any problems identified.

The DIRKS methodology and manual has been designed with flexibility in mind and allows you to use as much or as little of the methodology as you need to and as is relevant to your organization's EDRMS project. Fore more information regarding DIRKS, the full DIRKS methodology and manual can be found online at www.naa.gov.au/r ecordkeep-ing/dirks/dirksman/dirks.html.

MOREQ: Model Requirements for the Management of Electronic Records

MOREQ is a European standard for electronic records management (ERM) that was developed by the IDABC (Interoperable Delivery of European eGovernment Services to public Administrations, Businesses and Citizens). MOREQ, also referred to as Model Requirements, is a functional specification of the requirements for the management of electronic records. It is a functional specification that can be applied to both the public and private sectors as well electronic and manual (paper-based) records management systems.

The MOREQ specifications were developed in 2001, and the full specification consisting of 390 requirements and a 127-element metadata model is available to freely download from the IDABC Web site at http://europa.eu.int/idabc/en/document/2631/5585.

The MOREQ specification document provides a functional specification of all the major components of a records management system and includes separate chapter sections for classification schemes, controls and security, retention and disposal, capturing records, searching, retrieving and rendering, and administrative functions. Workflow, encryption, electronic signatures, and electronic watermarks are also covered in Chapter 10.

The MOREQ functional specification simply lists what an electronic records management system (ERMS) must do. Unlike ISO 15489 with DIRKS, there is not a similar kind of development methodology associated with the MOREQ functional specifications guide.

DoD 5015.2: Design Criteria Standard for ERM Software Applications

DoD 5015.2 is the U.S. Department of Defense (DoD) standard, aimed mainly at organizations related to the Department of Defense. The standard is a functional specification that prescribes mandatory functional requirements that ERMSs must meet to comply with the standard, based on and endorsed by the National Archives and Records Administration (NARA) regulations.

The DoD standard is used extensively in the United States as the benchmark for EDRM systems. Unlike ISO 15489, the DoD standard is purely a functional specification and does not include a development methodology such as DIRKS.

The documentation for the standard consists of four chapters. The first chapter is very small, and consists of just one page that describes the purpose and limitations of the standard. The second chapter lists the mandatory requirements that ERMSs must meet to comply with the standard. The third chapter lists the nonmandatory features of records management software. The fourth and final chapter discusses the management of classified records and the requirements records management software must meet in order to store and maintain classified records.

The mandatory requirements laid out in Chapter 2 of the standard cover the functionality concerning managing records, dates and date logic, implementing standard data (metadata), backward compatibility, accessibility, implementing file plans, retention and disposition, and filing e-mails, among other areas of functional requirements.

The nonmandatory requirements laid out in Chapter 3 cover storage availability, documentation, system performance, the hardware environment, operating system environment, the network environment, protocols such as TCP/IP and SMTP, e-mail interfaces, document management features, and workflow.

Further information can be obtained on the DoD 5015.2 and the standard downloaded from http://www.dtic.mil/whs/directives/corres/html/50152std.htm.

DoD 5015.2 — Compliant Systems

The Joint Interoperability Test Command (JITC) runs a software certification-testing program for EDRM systems that comply with the 5015.2 standard, which is endorsed by NARA. JITC maintain a product register of records management systems that have been tested and are compliant with DoD 5015.2. This register can be found online at http://jitc.fhu.disa.mil/recmgt/register.html. At the time of writing, this link is not active; however, it is possible to access this register through viewing cached copies held by Internet search engines.

The register is divided into two sections: those systems that are compliant with Chapter 4 of the standard concerning management of classified records, and those products that meet the requirements of the standard but do not meet the requirements laid down for classified records as described in Chapter 4 of the standard. Software that is currently certified also has a certification expiration date. Most of the major suppliers of EDRM software have obtained DoD 5015.2 compliance.

The National Archives–Compliant Systems (TNA 2002)

The National Archives in the United Kingdom, much the same as JITC in the United States, has evaluated EDRM systems and holds a list of approved suppliers and their products, which can be found at http://www.national-archives.gov.uk/electronicrecords/reqs2002/approved.htm. This set of functional requirements is commonly referred to as TNA 2002, where TNA is the abbreviation for The National Archives. The first version of TNA 2002 was published in 1999, but due to advances in both software and legislation, it was republished in 2002. The 2002 requirements take into account ISO 15489, MOREQ, the European standard for Model Requirements for ERM, the e-government interoperability framework in the United Kingdom incorporating the ERM metadata standard, the Freedom of Information Act 2000, and the Data Protection Act 1998.

The document that contains the functional requirements for ERMSs (TNA 2002) is divided into two sections — A and B. Section A sets out the core features that an ERMS must meet to comply with the functional requirements and be listed as an approved system by TNA. Section B sets out the optional requirements.

Among the core features set out in section A of the requirements is records organization, including classification schemes and file plans, class metadata, folders, folder metadata, and folder management. Other features include records capture, declaration and management, searching and displaying records, retention and disposal of records, access control, auditing, reporting, usability, design and performance, and compliance with other standards such as ISO 15489 Information and Documentation: Records Management. Section B is labeled optional modules, and includes authentication and encryption, electronic signatures and electronic watermarks, document management, and hybrid and physical folder management.

The functional requirements listed in TNA 2002 can be accessed at www.nationalarchives.gov.uk/electronicrecords/reqs2002.

Acts of Law

The following section of this chapter is concerned with legislation affecting ERM, especially holding information relating to individuals, as there are many Acts of Law that affect this, and they differ depending on the organization and country that the EDRM system is being implemented in.

Freedom of Information

Freedom of Information Acts exist in the vast majority of countries in the developed world and are currently being added to the statute books in many other developing countries. Freedom of information relates to the rights of both individuals and organizations to access information regarding almost any subject, provided that information is not subject to national security or of any other sensitive nature. For example, under the Freedom of Information Act, if an individual were to request that the local council or municipality office release all information held on him or her for the past 5 years, then the local council would be obliged by law to provide the citizen with this information within a given time period.

Freedom of Information requests can be made by virtually anybody to any organization, and the organization is obliged by law to provide this information. It is therefore necessary for the organization to have an adequate records management system in place to facilitate these requests for information.

Having an adequate EDRM system in place can mean the difference between clerical staff in an organization being able to perform a few searches to satisfy Freedom of Information requests within minutes or having to search for files in filing rooms and other physical locations in the organization, which may take hours or even days.

The Freedom of Information Act was enacted in the United States in 1966 and took effect on July 4, 1967; in the United Kingdom, the Freedom of Information Act 2000 came into force on January 1, 2005. There will of course be differences in the U.S. and U.K. Freedom of Information Acts as well among those in other countries. However, the basics principles of these Acts will be same, i.e., to provide access to the information.

The Privacy Act 1974 (United States) and Data Protection Act 1998 (United Kingdom)

The Acts are concerned with how information relating to individuals are stored within organizations, and lays down the procedures required for organization in storing and maintaining such information and the individuals' rights regarding access to the information.

The Privacy Act 1974 has been in effect in the United States since September 27, 1975, and the Data Protection Act 1998 came into force in the United Kingdom on March 1, 2000, amending and replacing the former Data Protection Act 1984.

Government Paperwork Elimination Act

The Government Paperwork Elimination Act is a U.S. law that took effect on October 21, 1998. The Act requires that all federal agencies, by 21 October 2003, allow individuals or organizations that deal with federal agencies the option of submitting information electronically, and it also puts the onus on federal agencies to hold all records electronically. The Act also states that electronic records and electronic signatures relating to those records will be legally admissible in a court of law.

Other Acts of Law and Regulations Impacting on Electronic Records

The Freedom of Information Act, the Data Protection Act, and The Privacy Act are particularly important in the context of EDRM systems, but they are not the only Acts of Law to state the importance of satisfactory records management.

Because records management affects every organization — right from a local convenience store to a multinational organization — there are Acts of Law relating to records management and recommendations for ERM made by regulatory organizations.

Other Acts of Law that state that organizations must maintain adequate and proper records management are the Sarbanes–Oxley Act 2002 and the Health Insurance Portability and Accountability Act (HIPAA). Regulatory organizations such as the U.S. Securities and Exchange Commission and the National Association of Security Dealers, among others, have also specified the need for adequate records management. The following are brief descriptions of other laws and regulations that impact on records management.

BSI PD 0008

BSI PD 0008 is a standard developed by the British Standards Institution (BSI) that is concerned with the "Legal Admissibility and Evidential Weight of Information Stored Electronically." The standard essentially relates to whether electronic documents and records have legal status and can be used in a court of law, and whether electronic documents have the same evidential weight as their paper counterparts. Thus, the standard is primarily concerned with the authenticity of electronic documents and records and storing them in such a way as to prove their authenticity.

The standard contains the following three parts:

- BIP 0008-1:2004 covers electronic storage of documents.
- BIP 0008-2:2005 covers documents communicated electronically (including e-mail).
- BIP 0008-3:2005 covers the linking of identity to an electronic document.

Part 1 of the code of practice, BIP 0008-1:2004, provides a framework and guidance that identify key areas of good practice for both the implementation and operation of electronic storage systems.

Part 2 of the code of practice, BIP 0008-2:2005, describes the procedures and processes for transferring electronic documents from one computer system to another, including e-mail, where the issues of authenticity and integrity of the transferred information are required to be legally admissible, providing evidential weight in a court of law. The code of practice refers to both documents sent and received, and to any documents or information sent between computer systems, such as e-mail, documents, messaging, etc.

Part 3 of the code of practice, BIP 0008-3:2005, details procedures concerning the use of digital certificates that can be used to identify individuals or organizations as the electronic equivalent of the individuals or organizations signing documents.

Each of the three codes of practice requires the organization to demonstrate and put in place certain procedures to demonstrate that good-practice procedures have been adhered to. These actions include the approval at board level of an Information Management Policy as well as an Information Security Policy.

The codes of practice also require that organizations consult with legal representatives and regulators to obtain approval for the electronic storage of information, as well as develop and document practices and procedures for users to follow, and that auditing facilities are available in order to provide audit trails for documents and records.

Health Insurance Portability and Accountability Act (HIPAA)

The Health Insurance Portability and Accountability Act 1996, known as HIPAA, came into force on October 16, 2003, in the United States, and lays down statutory obligations for healthcare providers to accept national standards for both electronic transactions and code sets, allowing payments to be made electronically between the healthcare insurance industry and hospitals and other medical practices.

HIPAA has specified that the healthcare industry use one format for making and receiving claims. It lays down complex and in-depth rules regarding privacy and security of information (documents and records) held within these information systems.

As for compliance, most of the larger EDRMS and ECM vendors offer HIPAA-compliant systems.

U.S. Securities and Exchange Commission

The U.S. Securities and Exchange Commission (SEC) was set up after the great stock market crash in 1929, its primary objective being to maintain and oversee the security markets and exchanges as well as to protect investors. The SEC is involved in the rule-making process that goes into maintaining and updating, as well as enforcing, Acts of Law that govern the securities and exchange markets in the United States. The Acts of Law that the SEC is responsible for enforcing are

- Securities Act of 1933
- Securities Exchange Act of 1934
- Public Utility Holding Company Act of 1935
- Trust Indenture Act of 1939

- Investment Company Act of 1940
- Investment Advisors Act of 1940
- Sarbanes–Oxley Act of 2002

These above Acts of Law as well as SEC rules are concerned with the proper recording of information (records) and the retention of records. An example of just two SEC rules is 17a-3 and 17a-4.

Rules 17a-3 and 17a-4 are concerned with the requirements for organizations that fall under the SEC to maintain and retain records using specific methods for a specific period in time. Both fall under the Securities Exchange Act of 1934.

There have been incidents where noncompliance with SEC rules have resulted in extremely large fines running into millions of dollars. However, most of the large EDRMS and ECM software vendors offer products and solutions that are compliant with SEC and other financial laws and regulations. Further information on the U.S. Securities and Exchange Commission can be found online at http://www.sec.gov.

National Association of Security Dealers

The National Association of Security Dealers (NASD) is a self-regulating organization made up of members from the security and exchanges industry, such as brokerage firms and stockbrokers. As a self-regulating organization, NASD creates and enforces rules for it members based on the Federal Securities laws previously mentioned. The SEC oversees the NASD and approves rules made by the latter.

As with the SEC, many of the rules made by the NASD relate to proper record-keeping methods. For example, Rule 3100, Books and Records, requires members to keep and maintain books and records in keeping with all laws and regulations and as determined by SEC Rules 17a-3 and 17a-4. Rule 3110 also requires members of NASD to maintain customer account information to a prescribed method as defined by Rule 3110. Further information on NASD and the rules governing it member organizations can be found online at http://www.nasd.com.

Financial Services and Markets Act 2000

The Financial Services Authority (FSA), the United Kingdom equivalent of both SEC and NASD in the United States, are responsible for enforcing the rules of the Financial Services and Markets Act 2000, and under Section 153 of the Act, the FSA is to create and publish a list of rules that is referred to as the FSA Handbook.

The FSA Handbook includes recommendations on document and records management, with Rule 5.3.1 (6) requiring that organizations need to retain all accounting records for a minimum period of six years. The rule also requires that, for the first two years, accounting records need to be stored using a method whereby they are available, and can be produced, within 24 hr of request.

Further information on the Financial Services and Markets Act 2000 and the implications the Act has for financial services organizations can be found online at the Financial Services Authority Web site, www.fsa.gov.uk.

Sarbanes–Oxley Act

The Sarbanes–Oxley Act came into force in 2002 in the United States. It focuses on greater corporate regulations and introduces more stringent accounting practices for U.S. organizations. The Act came about after the collapse of several major international U.S.-based organizations that became insolvent due to accounting irregularities and malpractice.

One of the Act's primary objectives is to protect investors by focusing on greater corporate disclosure and transparency. IT and Information Systems play a significant role in the enforcement of the Act, and it requires that organizations document the IT and Information Systems procedures and controls they have in place in order to ensure compliance.

One of the most important aspects of the Act in relation to IT and Information Systems is Section 404, which is primarily concerned with the authenticity of the information, especially relating to the accounts and auditing procedures of the organization. Failure to comply with the Act includes heavy financial penalties or even jail time for corporate officers signing off on the corporate accounts.

International Financial Reporting Standards

These standards are the result of a decade-long initiative that aims to standardize the core elements of accounting methods used around the world. From 2006 onwards, most major businesses in Europe will have adopted the International Financial Reporting Standards and use its methods for submitting their accounts. This will involve organizations disclosing a greater depth of financial information, ensuring that certain items appear on balance sheets in a consistent fashion. This, in turn, will put the onus on the individual departments and business units to supply their organizations' accounting teams with greater information, obtained in the vast majority of cases from the organizations' information management systems, which also include the both EDRMS and ECM systems.

The e-Privacy Directive

The e-Privacy Directive became law in the United Kingdom in October 2003. The law is concerned with organizations' use of electronic communication for direct marketing purposes. The electronic communication methods the law covers are phone calls, e-mails, and interactions between the organizations' Web sites and Web site visitors.

The e-Privacy Directive requires organizations that engage in direct marketing activities to secure personal and behavioral data such as caller ID and locations. It also specifies that recipients have the right to refuse cookies being installed on their PCs in order to access organizations' Web sites. Organizations also have to secure the permission of recipients before sending them direct-marketing e-mails.

Environmental Information Regulations 2004

The Environmental Information Regulations 2004 (EIR) came into force in the United Kingdom on January 1, 2005, which coincided with the Freedom of Information Act 2000. Like the Freedom of Information Act, the Environmental Information Regulations state that the public has access to environmental information held by public authorities and certain other organizations. However, unlike the U.K. Freedom of Information request, requests under the Environmental Information Regulations do not need to be put in writing. Anyone can simply request environmental information on any element of the environment such as land, water, and biological organisms, as well as information regarding the economic impact and analysis of activities that affect the environment. Further information on the Environmental Information Regulations can be found on the DEFRA Web site, available at http://www.defra.gov.uk.

Conclusion

As discussed in this chapter, there are many Acts of Law and Regulations concerning the storage of documents and records. A number of these Acts and Regulations are concerned with the authenticity of records. Acts such as the Freedom of Information, Data Protection, and Privacy Act are common to all organizations, whereas ones such as the Health Insurance Portability and Accountability Act and Financial Services and Markets Act are generally only relevant to their respective industries. However, the latter could also apply to organizations that, though not falling within the respective industries, may interact with those that do, such as Healthcare or Financial Services.

The issue of compliance with laws and regulations is an important and complicated matter that needs to be thoroughly examined by suitably qualified personnel, such as legal advisors and attorneys, before any systems are procured and implemented. Luckily, most of the larger vendors of EDRMS solutions offer specific solutions for specific industries that are compliant with all the laws and regulations relating to those industries.

Part 2

COMPONENTS
OF EDRMS

Chapter 4

Creating Electronic Document Types

Documents types are the electronic means of storing documents as electronic images, as well as the associated information regarding the document that would effectively index the document and categorize it, allowing it to be stored in an ordered manner within the EDRMS.

Electronic documents contain indexing information, often referred to as metadata, as well as an image of the paper document. The metadata will index and categorize the document, allowing for indexed storage, thereby allowing for easier and more precise retrieval of the document. The indexing and categorization of the electronic document would contain information such as the type of document, the date the document was created, the date the document was filed, and other information depending on the exact document types and indexing requirements. The image of the document could be as little as one page to many pages in length.

Gathering Requirements for Defining Electronic Documents

In order to gather requirements for defining electronic document types, you will need to liaise heavily with users in the organization. The requirements-gathering exercise is a crucial point in defining the EDRMS because the way in which documents are indexed and categorized is crucial to their storage and retrieval.

To illustrate the kind of document indexing and categorizing, let us consider a planning application document type. A planning application would have the following information associated with it, such as the applicant's name and address, an agent's name and address, and the date. This can be broken down into a table of fields that would accept certain types of data as illustrated in Figure 4.1.

The rest of this chapter will present a stepped approach that can be taken to gather electronic document type requirements that results in defining the individual document types with metadata. Such requirements will be based on the needs of an environmental services department within a city council or municipality office.

Field Name	Data Type	Length	Format
Applicant Title	Alphanumeric	10	
Applicant Forename	Alphanumeric	100	
Applicant Surname	Alphanumeric	100	
Applicant Initials	Alphanumeric	10	
Applicant Address Line 1	Alphanumeric	100	
Applicant Address Line 2	Alphanumeric	100	
Applicant Address Line 3	Alphanumeric	100	
Applicant Address 4	Alphanumeric	100	
Applicant Address 5	Alphanumeric	100	
Applicant Address 6	Alphanumeric	100	
Applicant Postal Code / Zip Code	Alphanumeric	10	
Agent Company Name	Alphanumeric	100	
Agent Contact Person Title	Alphanumeric	10	
Agent Contact Person Surname	Alphanumeric	10	
Agent Contact Person Forename	Alphanumeric	100	
Agent Address Line 1	Alphanumeric	100	
Agent Address Line 2	Alphanumeric	100	
Agent Address Line 3	Alphanumeric	100	
Agent Address Line 4	Alphanumeric	100	
Agent Address Line 5	Alphanumeric	100	
Agent Address Line 6	Alphanumeric	100	
Agent Postal Code / Zip Code	Alphanumeric	10	
Date of Planning Application	Date		mm/dd/yyyy
Date Document Filed	Date		mm/dd/yyyy

Figure 4.1 Planning application document metadata.

Defining Electronic Document Types

Step 1 — Working with a Representative Cross Section of the Department

The first step in defining electronic document types is to gather together a cross section of users from the department. They should range from junior clerical staff to senior management within the department, as this will ensure that the entire department's needs are met for all staff working in it.

Step 2 — Discovering the Department's Main Activities

One of the best approaches to take in defining the document types would be to run a workshop where business analysts could first gather requirements by asking the staff to bring along samples of paper documents for each of their respective activities. The idea behind this is to extract a list of activities that the department carries out. These activities can then be translated into the document groups for each section of the department.

A typical environmental services department would normally cover the following range of activities: food, health and safety, pest control, pollution, recycling, refuse collection, public conveniences, and street cleansing, among others. This list is shown in Figure 4.2 as document groups for environmental services. Thus, to sum up, each departmental activity such as food, health and safety, pollution, refuse collection, etc., maps directly to a document group.

- Food
- Health and safety
- Pest control
- Pollution
- Recycling
- Refuse collection
- Public conveniences
- Street cleansing

Figure 4.2 Main document groups for environmental services.

Step 3 — Defining Document Types for Each Document Group

Once the list of document groups has been compiled, as shown in Figure 4.2, the business analyst can start to work with key users in each document group (departmental activity), such as food or health and safety to determine the requirements for individual document types within each document group. This is to determine the different types of paper documents that each document group has both in their folders and in use on a daily basis. Examples of document types relating to health and safety would be letters, applications, notices, accidents, near misses, etc. Once this list is defined for each document group, then you will have the start of the individual document types for each group. A list of document types for each document group is shown in Figure 4.3.

Document Groups	Document Types
Food	Applications
	Letters
	Notices
	Reports
	Contracts
Health and safety	Accidents
	Applications
	Letters
	Notices
	Reports
	Contracts
Pest control	Letters
	Notices
	Contracts
Pollution	Letters
	Notices
	Reports
	Contracts

Figure 4.3   Document types for each document group.

Document Groups	Document Types
Recycling	Letters
	Notices
	Reports
	Contracts
Refuse collection	Letters
	Notices
	Reports
	Contracts
Public conveniences	Letters
	Notices
	Reports
	Contracts
Street cleansing	Letters
	Notices
	Reports
	Contracts

Figure 4.3 Document types for each document group (continued).

Step 4 — Defining Metadata for Each Document Type

Now that we have a list of document types for each document group, we can finalize the definition of each individual document type by deciphering the metadata that needs to be associated with the document type in order to categorize and index a document within the EDRMS.

When defining metadata for document types, it is best to work with the staff that manage and are responsible for those paper documents you will be defining the metadata for. Working from the paper documents, you should quite easily be able to figure out what extra data is needed to index the documents. Figure 4.4 displays an example Health and Safety Accident Form.

Health and Safety at Work etc Act 1974 **?**
The Reporting of Injuries, Diseases and Dangerous Occurrences Regulations 1995

HSE
Health & Safety
Executive

Click here for report guidance

Report of an injury or dangerous occurrence

Filling in this form
This form must be filled in by an employer or other responsible person.

Part A

About you

1 What is your full name?

2 What is your job title?

3 What is your telephone number?

About your organisation

4 What is the name of your organisation?

5 What is its address and postcode?

6 What type of work does the organisation do?

Part B

About the incident

1 On what date did the incident happen?

2 At what time did the incident happen?
(Please use the 24-hour clock eg 0600)

3 Did the incident happen at the above address?

Yes ☐ Go to question 4

No ☐ Where did the incident happen?

☐ elsewhere in your organisation – give the name, address and postcode
☐ at someone else's premises – give the name, address and postcode
☐ in a public place – give details of where it happened

If you do not know the postcode, what is the name of the local authority?

4 In which department, or where on the premises, did the incident happen?

F2508 (05.00)

Part C

About the injured person

If you are reporting a dangerous occurrence, go to Part F. If more than one person was injured in the same incident, please attach the details asked for in Part C and Part D for each injured person.

1 What is their full name?

2 What is their home address and postcode?

3 What is their home phone number?

4 How old are they?

5 Are they
☐ male?
☐ female?

6 What is their job title?

7 Was the injured person (tick only one box)
☐ one of your employees?
☐ on a training scheme? Give details:

☐ on work experience?
☐ employed by someone else? Give details of the employer:

☐ self-employed and at work?
☐ a member of the public?

Part D

About the injury

1 What was the injury? (eg fracture, laceration)

2 What part of the body was injured?

Next Page

Figure 4.4   Report of an injury or dangerous occurrence.

3 Was the injury (tick the one box that applies)

☐ a fatality?

☐ a major injury or condition? (see accompanying notes)

☐ an injury to an employee or self-employed person which prevented them doing their normal work for more than 3 days?

☐ an injury to a member of the public which meant they had to be taken from the scene of the accident to a hospital for treatment?

4 Did the injured person (tick all the boxes that apply)

☐ become unconscious?

☐ need resuscitation?

☐ remain in hospital for more than 24 hours?

☐ none of the above.

Part E

About the kind of accident

Please tick the one box that best describes what happened, then go to Part G.

☐ Contact with moving machinery or material being machined

☐ Hit by a moving, flying or falling object

☐ Hit by a moving vehicle

☐ Hit something fixed or stationary

☐ Injured while handling, lifting or carrying

☐ Slipped, tripped or fell on the same level

☐ Fell from a height

How high was the fall?

| metres |

☐ Trapped by something collapsing

☐ Drowned or asphyxiated

☐ Exposed to, or in contact with, a harmful substance

☐ Exposed to fire

☐ Exposed to an explosion

☐ Contact with electricity or an electrical discharge

☐ Injured by an animal

☐ Physically assaulted by a person

☐ Another kind of accident (describe it in Part G)

Part F

Dangerous occurrences

Enter the number of the dangerous occurrence you are reporting. (The numbers are given in the Regulations and in the notes which accompany this form)

For official use

Client number	Location number	Event number

☐ INV REP ☐ Y ☐ N

Part G

Describing what happened

Give as much detail as you can. For instance

- the name of any substance involved
- the name and type of any machine involved
- the events that led to the incident
- the part played by any people.

If it was a personal injury, give details of what the person was doing. Describe any action that has since been taken to prevent a similar incident. Use a separate piece of paper if you need to.

Part H

Your signature

Signature

Date

Where to send the form
Incident Contact Centre, Caerphilly Business Centre, Caerphilly Business Park, Caerphilly, CF83 3GG, or email to riddor@natbrit.com or fax to 0845 300 99 24

If returning by post/fax, please ensure this form is signed, alternatively, if returning by E-Mail, please type your name in the signature box

Continue

Figure 4.4   Report of an injury or dangerous occurrence (continued).

Defining Metadata for Searching and Retrieval Methods

The reason for defining metadata to associate with the document is that the document can be indexed and categorized in an ordered manner. However, the ultimate reason for indexing and categorizing the document in an ordered manner is so that we can search for and retrieve the document at a later date after the document has already been indexed, categorized, and archived in the system. Having the correct metadata fields and values associated with the document will allow the user to quickly locate all documents relating to a particular incident. For example, let's say you need to quickly find all Health and Safety Accident documents relating to Fred Smith. Then, if the Health and Safety Accident documents had been indexed and categorized with the associated metadata of at least surname and forename, then a user of the system could perform a search specifying a surname of "Smith" and a forename of "Fred" in the metadata values. As long as the documents had been archived into the system accurately with the correct surname and forename values of "Smith" and "Fred," respectively, the user's search would return all documents with these metadata values, i.e., all documents relating to Fred Smith.

Defining Metadata for the Health and Safety Accident Document

The Health and Safety Accident form shown in Figure 4.4 has eight sections, labeled Part A through Part H. Each part of the form, together with description of the information required, is shown in Figure 4.5.

A good place to start with the definition of metadata for the Health and Safety Accident document is to look at the mandatory fields in the document. These are fields that simply must have text entered in them for the completed form to be accepted.

Another good starting point is looking at each part of the form in turn to analyze and decide what information would prove useful for categorizing and indexing the document, as well as searching and retrieving the document after it has been indexed and categorized. For example, do you want to be able to group certain types of accidents together such as electrical accidents? If this was the case, then you need to specify a mandatory metadata field such as "accident type," which consisted of preselected accident types, such as electrical accidents, falls, near-misses, etc., which would be specified by the user. This would then enable a user searching specific kinds of accidents such as electrical accidents to simply select the metadata value of electrical accidents on the search form and retrieve all accident forms that relate to electrical accidents in the returned search results.

Part A	About you contains information regarding the person who is reporting the accident, since this person may well be a different person to the injured person
Part B	About the Incident; contains information about the incident
Part C	About the injured person; contains information about the injured person
Part D	About the Injury; contains information regarding the injury
Part E	About the kind of accident, contains a series of tick boxes where the person who is filling in the form is asked to tick just one box that best describes what happened
Part F	Dangerous occurrences asks the person who is filling in the form to enter the number of dangerous occurrences that have happened
Part G	Describing what happened; contains a free text box where the people filling in the form can describe what happened in their own words
Part H	Your signature, simply asks for the signature of the person who is filling in the form and the date

Figure 4.5   Description of Health and Safety Accident Form parts.

Using Mandatory Fields to Define Metadata

The mandatory fields are shown in bold on the Health and Safety Accident document shown in Figure 4.4, and only the mandatory fields are shown

About you:
- What is your full name?
- What is your job title?
- What is your telephone number?

About your organization:
- What is the name of your organization?
- What is its address and postcode?
- What type of work does the organization do?

About the incident:
- On what date did the incident happen?
- At what time did the incident happen?
- In which department, or where on the premises did the incident happen?

Figure 4.6   List of mandatory fields in the Health and Safety Accident Form.

in Figure 4.6. Using these questions and a basic knowledge of defining database tables will assist you in defining the metadata for this document.

The first question is, "What is your name?" The metadata fields for this question would translate into Surname, Firstname, and Initials because we would want to be able to search for the document using either someone's surname and/or their forename and/or even their initials.

Note: The trick here is to think ahead about how you would like to search for the document because, as mentioned previously, the way the document is categorized and indexed and the metadata associated with it defines how users are able to search for the document.

The next question, "What is your job title?" would simply translate into the metadata field of "Job Title." "What is your telephone number?" translates into "telephone number."

In the section "About your organization," there are three questions that need to be translated into metadata fields. The first question, "What is the name of your organization?" simply translates into "Organization Name." The next question, "What is its address and postcode," can be converted into a metadata field using one of three possible methods.

The first approach to convert "What is its address and postcode" would be to simply convert the question into one metadata field of "Organization Address." The issue with converting the question into just one metadata field is that it would make it harder to distinguish the address from the postcode or zip code, thereby making searching for an organization more difficult.

The second approach would be to create two metadata fields, one labeled "address" and the other labeled "postcode" or "zip code." This would make it easier to search for an organization using its address because it will allow you to specify part of or all of the address, and part of or the entire postcode or zip code.

The third approach would be to create metadata fields consisting of separate address lines, say, from Address 1 through to Address 6, as well as a separate field for postcode or zip code. Although this approach would provide for a thoroughly indexed document, it could make searching using the address much harder. For example, if a user knew that part of the address for the organization they wanted to search for contained the word "The Parade," then, to search for the part of the address "The Parade," the user would need to know in which address field the "The Parade" was in, as it could be in Address Line 1 or Address Line 2 or Address Line 3 or any other address line. To compensate for this, the search could search all of the address fields for "The Parade," but this approach often slows down searches, making the retrieval when searching for documents that much longer.

The best approach to defining the metadata of the address and postcode of the organization would be to specify just a single address field and also a single postcode field as this would give a balance between specifically indexing the document with the address and postcode and providing for efficient and effective searching.

The question "What type of work does the organization do?" could simply be converted to a metadata field of "Organization's business type" or something similar to describe the type of work the organization undertakes.

The next section, titled "About the incident," asks the person who is filling in the form the date the incident happened, the time the incident happened, and where the incident happened. These questions can quite easily be converted to metadata fields of "Incident Date," "Incident Time," and "Incident Location (Department/Premises)."

Specifying Metadata Field Types

We now have some of the main metadata field names defined. However, we have not yet defined the metadata fields in terms of field types, field length, and field format. Again, this is where a basic understanding of defining database tables comes into play. Metadata fields that require the user to enter information such as surname and firstname need to accept alphanumeric characters as well as being a minimum length of 50 characters, in order to accommodate the longest of both firstnames and surnames. The Initials field, again, needs to be of the type alphanumeric and will need to be up to five characters in length to accept possibly the longest of initials.

Metadata fields that accept telephone numbers can be specified as the field type alphanumeric but will need to be formatted in order to accept only numbers where the numbers that make up the telephone number exist. For example, let's say the telephone number the user was going to enter would be 1-999-123-4567, then the formatting for this metadata field would be n-nnn-nnn-nnnn, where n stands for numerical character. The reason why the telephone number is specified as alphanumeric and not numeric is because you do not use telephone numbers for summing up, i.e., in math, and also there needs to be additional symbols apart from the numbers 1–9 contained within the field. The length of the telephone number field will depend upon the country in which the system is being implemented and that country's format and length of telephone numbers.

Metadata fields that accept dates should be specified as date field types and also should be formatted in the date format for the country in which the system is being implemented. For example, in the United States, the date formatting would be mm-dd-yyyy, and in the United Kingdom, the date formatting would be dd-mm-yyyy. Fields that accept the time should be specified as time fields, and should be formatted according to the 24-hr clock as hh:mm:ss. Figure 4.7 displays the full definition for the metadata field derived from the mandatory fields of the Health and Safety Accident form.

Analyzing Each Part of the Form to Derive Metadata

By examining the mandatory fields of the Health and Safety Accident form and converting these into corresponding metadata fields, we have made a start in defining the metadata for the document. However, by taking a closer look at each section of the form, we would be able to derive further metadata that would be useful in indexing the document. We need to refer to the Health and Safety Accident form as shown in Figure 4.4.

Part A — About You

By looking at Part A of the form, we can see that we have already covered the six mandatory questions in the previous section.

Part B — About the Incident

Looking at Part B of the form, we can see that there are four questions, three of them mandatory. The three mandatory questions have been

Field Name	Field Type	Field Length	Formatting
Surname	Alphanumeric	50	
Forename	Alphanumeric	50	
Initials	Alphanumeric	5	
Job Title	Alphanumeric	50	
Telephone Number	Alphanumeric	Depends upon the country's telephone number length	Depends on the country's telephone number format
Organization Name	Alphanumeric	50	
Organization Address	Alphanumeric	500	
Organization Postcode	Alphanumeric	Depends upon the country's post code / zip code length	Depends upon the country's post code / zip code length
Organization Business Type	Alphanumeric	50	
Incident Date	Date	8	Depends upon the country's date format, e.g. - dd-mm-yyyy, mm-dd-yyyy
Incident Time	Time	8	Hh:mm:ss (24-hour clock format should be used)
Incident Location (Department / Premises)	Alphanumeric	100	

Figure 4.7   Metadata definitions for the mandatory fields of the Health and Safety Accident Form.

covered in the previous section. Question B.3 asks if the incident happened at the above address.

We need to ask ourselves if creating a metadata field for this question would help to index the document or if it would be useful in reporting procedures. With regard to indexing the document, there would not be much benefit arrived through creating this metadata field. However, with regard to reporting, especially if the organization wanted to run reports specifying where accidents occurred in the context of who reported them, then creating this metadata field would come in quite useful because the reporting program could simply look at the metadata field and count up how many injuries or dangerous occurrences occurred within the organization, occurred in an organization different from the reporting organization, or occurred in a public place.

A good rule of thumb to follow in deciding whether or not to create metadata fields is, "if in doubt, create the metadata field," as it can be created as a discretionary field, i.e., a field that does not need to be completed. It is also much harder to add an extra metadata field to the document type after the document type has been created because this would mean re-indexing all previously indexed documents, and because the information is stored within the document, every document that was previously indexed would need to be opened, read, and then the metadata field value selected or entered in manually, which amounts to a time-intensive and laborious process.

In the case of the metadata field questioning whether the incident happened at the above address, the metadata field can be created and labeled as "Did the incident occur at the address mentioned above?" As this is a question that can be answered with a yes/no answer, then the metadata field type would be boolean, allowing the person who is entering data on the form to select Yes/No. If the user selects Yes, then no further information would be required regarding this question. However, if the user entered No, then a further three questions need to be presented to the user, and the first question needs to be mandatory.

The first question would ask the user to select where the incident occurred from a list of three selections. These selections would be labeled "Elsewhere in your organization," "At someone else's premises," or "A public place." Two more metadata fields would also need to be presented to the user, labeled "Incident Address and Postcode" and "Incident Local Authority." The metadata field asking for the "Incident Address and Postcode" should be mandatory, but the metadata field "Incident Local Authority" should be discretionary because it does not need to be filled in if the person who filled in the form has entered the address and postcode of the incident, and also the local authority may not be known by the person who is filling in the form.

Part C — About the Injured Person

Part C asks a series of questions about the injured person. These questions are not mandatory on the form, but each provides useful information. Again, we have to ask the question "Will the definition of metadata for these questions help with either indexing the document or with reporting or statistics?"

Question C.1 asks for the injured person's full name. We have already defined metadata for surname, forename and initials in the previous section, using mandatory fields to define metadata.

However, the surname, firstname, and initials relate to the name of the person reporting the incident, and this name is the name of the injured person. We now need a way to distinguish the difference between these two names. We can create metadata fields for the injured person's name and label them injured person surname, injured person forename, and injured person initials. We still need to modify, though, the labels for the existing surname, forename, and initials metadata fields to make them more descriptive and unambiguous. A solution would be to relabel the surname, forename, and initials fields in Part A as "Reporting Party Surname," "Reporting Party Forename," and "Reporting Party Initials." All these fields should be mandatory.

Question C.2 asks for the injured person's home address and postcode. As with previous address and postcode questions, we can create two new metadata fields, one for address and one for postcode. In this case, we would need to label them "Injured Person's Address" and "Injured Person's Postcode," respectively, and both these fields need to be mandatory.

Question C.3 asks for the injured person's home phone number. Although this field is very useful to the report form, it is not useful in indexing the document or for reporting purposes, so we do not need to create a metadata field for this question.

Question C.4 asks, "How old is the person?" Again this field is not useful in indexing the document or for reporting purposes.

Question C.5 asks for the injured person's sex. Although this field would not be of any use in indexing the document, it would be useful with reporting and statistics, and therefore we would create a metadata field labeled "Injured Person's Sex." This field should be made mandatory.

Question C.6 asks the injured person's job title, and question C.7 asks for the specific questions about the job role of the injured person. These questions do not have any bearing on indexing the document or reporting matters, and therefore metadata fields are not created for them.

Part D — About the Injury

Part D asks for specific information regarding the injury. These questions would be quite useful for indexing the document and could also be used in reporting and statistical analysis of injuries and dangerous occurrences.

Question D.1 asks, "What was the injury?" Question D.2 asks "What part of the body was injured?" These questions would not add any value to indexing the document, and because they are free text fields allowing the person who is filling in the report to enter almost any description, they cannot be used for reporting, and therefore we do not convert these fields into metadata fields.

Question D.3 asks, "What was the injury?" and asks the person who is filling in the form to tick the one box that applies. This field would be very useful for reporting purposes, and therefore we can create a metadata field labeled "Injury Type" as a drop-down list box allowing the user to select one of the possible answers as specified on the form.

Question D.4 asks if the injured person suffered certain conditions, and asks the person who is filling in the form to tick all the boxes that apply. Again, this field would be quite useful for reporting purposes, and therefore a metadata field labeled "Injured Person's Condition" could be created. This metadata field could then be presented with either four check boxes or a select list allowing the user to select one or more of the options.

Part E — About the Kind of Accident

Part E asks the person who is filling in the form to tick one box that best describes the kind of accident that happened. As this would be a useful feature to be able to report on, we can create a metadata field labeled "Type of Accident" and present it as a drop-down list for the user to choose one type of injury.

Part F — Dangerous Occurrences

This section asks the user to enter the number of dangerous occurrences they are reporting. As this question has no bearing on either indexing the document and reporting, there is no need to create a metadata field for it.

Part G — Describing What Happened

In this section of the form the user is asked to describe what happened in as much detail as possible. This field essentially contains the main content of the document and cannot be translated into a metadata field. However, if this main section of the document has been typed as opposed to handwritten, the typed content can be indexed using OCR (Optical Character Recognition), allowing for the content to be searched. Searching and OCR will be covered in greater depth in Chapter 7.

What Other Documents Would Be Related to This Type of Document?

Now that we have defined metadata for the health and safety document both by looking at the mandatory fields of the document and analyzing each part of the document, we now need to consider which other documents would be related to this document and how those documents could be linked to this.

Documents such as letters, reports, notices, and even applications could be linked to this document. One possible solution for creating a link between the health and safety form and the documents mentioned previously could be to create a reference number metadata field. The reference number could be assigned to the documents as they are indexed on to the system, thereby effectively grouping all documents together under a common and unique reference number for the particular case.

Standard Metadata Fields

The document date is a standard metadata field that needs to be added to every single document regardless. Another standard metadata field is creator. The creator metadata field contains the name of the person who has created or indexed the document. Together with document date, these two metadata fields provide information regarding who inputted the document and on what date, which is absolutely essential when it comes to auditing documents and producing audit trails.

The Completed Metadata Definition

Now that we have analyzed the health and safety form in terms of both mandatory fields and each part of the form, we have a complete definition of the metadata required, which is shown in Figure 4.8.

The completed metadata definition can also quite easily be converted into a form on the computer screen, in which users can enter the metadata values when indexing the document, as shown in Figure 4.9.

Field Name	Field Type	Field Length	Formatting	Mandatory
Reporting Person's Surname	Alphanumeric	50		Yes
Reporting Person's Forename	Alphanumeric	50		Yes
Reporting Person's Initials	Alphanumeric	5		Yes
Job Title	Alphanumeric	50		Yes
Telephone Number	Alphanumeric	Depends upon the country's telephone number length	Depends upon the country's telephone number format	Yes
Organization Name	Alphanumeric	50		Yes
Organization Address	Alphanumeric	500		Yes
Organization Postcode	Alphanumeric	Depends upon the country's post code/ zip code length	Depends upon the country's post code/ zip code length	Yes
Organization Business Type	Alphanumeric	50		Yes
Incident Date	Date	8	Depends upon the country's date format, e.g., dd-mm-yyyy, mm-dd-yyyy	Yes
Incident Time	Time	8	hh:mm:ss (24-hour clock format should be used)	Yes
Incident Location (Department/ Premises)	Alphanumeric	100		Yes

Figure 4.8   Complete metadata definitions for the Health and Safety Accident document.

Field Name	Field Type	Field Length	Formatting	Mandatory
Did the incident occur at the address mentioned above	Boolean	1		Yes
Elsewhere in your organization	Boolean	1		
At someone else's premises	Boolean	1		
A public place	Boolean	1		
Incident Address and Postcode	Alphanumeric	500		
Incident Local Authority	Alphanumeric	100		
Reporting Party Surname	Alphanumeric	100		Yes
Reporting Party Forename	Alphanumeric	100		Yes
Reporting Party Initials	Alphanumeric	100		Yes
Injured Person's Address	Alphanumeric	500		Yes
Injured Person's Postcode	Alphanumeric	15		Yes
Injured Person's Sex	Alphanumeric	6	Drop down list — Choice between male or female	Yes
Injury Type	Alphanumeric		Drop down list of values	
Injured Person's Condition	Alphanumeric		4 check boxes	
Type of Injury	Alphanumeric		Drop down list of values	

Figure 4.8   Complete metadata definitions for the Health and Safety Accident document (continued).

Reporting Person's Surname	
Reporting Person's Forename	
Reporting Person's Initials	
Job Title	
Telephone Number	
Organization Name	
Organization Address	
Organization Postcode	
Organization Business Type	
Incident Date	
Incident Time	
Incident Location (Department/Premises)	
Did the incident occur at the address mentioned above	☐
Elsewhere in your organization	☐
At someone else's premises	☐
A public place	☐
Incident Address and Postcode	
Incident Local Authority	
Reporting Party Surname	
Reporting Party Forename	
Reporting Party Initials	
Injured Person's Address	
Injured Person's Postcode	
Injured Person's Sex	Male ▼
Injury Type	Fatality ▼
Injured Person's Condition	☐ Become Unconscious ☐ Need resuscitation ☐ Remain in hospital for more than 24 hours ☐ None of the above
Type of Accident	Contact with moving machinery or material being ▼

Figure 4.9   Form for indexing health and safety form.

Letters

Letters are a document type that all departments will use. We can therefore define a standard letter document type with metadata that can be utilized to allow users to classify and index letters for storage in the systems document repository.

Field Name	Field Type	Field Length	Formatting	Mandatory
From Forename	Alphanumeric	50		No
From Surname	Alphanumeric	50		No
From Company	Alphanumeric	100		No
Your Ref	Alphanumeric	50		No
Our Ref	Alphanumeric	50		No
Description	Alphanumeric	100		No
Date	Alphanumeric	8	Depends on country	Yes

Figure 4.10   Metadata definition for a standard letter document type.

Some letters will be connected with other documents. This is where the reference number metadata field comes in, allowing users to assign the same reference number to a new letter, or allowing them to use another method to enable them link a letter or other document to an existing document or record.

Note: Ideally, the EDRM system should allow a user to search for an existing document or record within the system to link to a new letter or document, too, using a point-and-click method, as this would eliminate manual typing errors.

Metadata fields for a standard letter document type that would cover most departments is shown in Figure 4.10.

Uploading Files from Other Sources

There is also a need to upload straight from external sources such as mobile phones, digital cameras, and PDAs. This type of data could include simple text documents consisting of notes, sound recordings, images, or video clips from digital cameras or cellular phones, among others.

A document type will need to be created for this information as well as for linking this information to existing documents and records. This document type will also need to be named. A possible name could be "extra information" because it will primarily contain extra information that is connected to other documents.

For example, if a local council/municipality officer went out to investigate an alleged case of fly tipping, then the officer could take a picture

Field Name	Field Type	Field Length	Formatting	Mandatory
Description	Alphanumeric	100		Yes
Date	Alphanumeric	8	Depends on country	Yes

Figure 4.11   Metadata definition for Extra-Information document type.

of the scene using a digital camera. The image from the digital camera would then need to be uploaded into the document repository and would be regarded as extra information connected to an existing document or could be used as extra information (evidence) in a new document or report. Because the extra information document type covers a variety of different file types and is attached to other documents and records instead of being a document or record in its own right, it only needs to consist of two mandatory fields — Description and Date — as shown in Figure 4.11.

Creating Document Types for the Other Departments

Now that we have created the document type and defined its associated metadata for the health and safety accident report, we can use the same method in creating documents types and defining metadata for all the other documents in the organization that need to be converted to electronic document types. It's simply a matter of analyzing each paper-based document used in each department and defining its electronic counterpart using the steps and methods discussed in this chapter.

Chapter 5

Creating the Folder Structure

Now that we have defined the electronic document types and document groups, we can create the folder structure that will be used in the document repository to store an organization's electronic documents and records.

The folder structure should be created as a hierarchical structure containing different levels that effectively group the different sections of the organization's documents and records together. As with creating the electronic document groups and document types, we can use a similar stepped approach to creating the folder structure. However, we need to consider how documents may relate to properties or businesses, and how certain documents may relate to a certain case or incident. Hence, there are different approaches we can take in defining the folder structure.

Folder structures need to be created in an intuitive and easy-to-browse manner, which will aid users in locating documents and records. In order to create the folder structure in such a manner, you should consider how the organization currently files paper-based documents and records. Most organizations will store paper-based documents and records along some kind of organizational structure, with each department in the organization storing its own files and folders. Depending on the department's activities, files and folders may be stored against client names — both businesses and individuals — stored against property addresses, or stored against projects. All these factors have to be taken into account when creating the folder structure.

The Organizational Structure

Creating a folder structure that maps on to the existing organizational structure is one approach we can take in defining the folder structure. It is relatively straightforward to create because the folder structure that is created within the document repository is the same as the organizational structure.

The disadvantage with creating a folder structure using this method is that if the organization's structure changes, i.e., the organization goes through restructuring, then the folder structure that has been originally created will become out of date and, as time passes after the organizational restructuring, the folder structure defined in the document repository will become harder to use. Eventually, it will start not to make sense to the users of the system. However, most organizations only go through restructuring processes once every few years, so, in the event that an organization did go through restructuring, folders, documents, and records could be migrated to reflect the new organizational structure.

In defining the folder structure along the lines of the organizational structure, we need to start by creating a top-level folder that represents the organization and is the container for all other folders. We would then create second-level folders underneath the top-level folder, which would be the same as the departments within the organization, for example, Environmental Services, Planning Services, Building Services, etc. Then, within each of the second-level departmental folders, we would create third-level folders that map on to the documents group, which in turn represent the specific teams within the department. Referring back to Chapter 4, Environmental Services document groups would be Food, Health and Safety, Pest Control, Pollution, Recycling, Refuse Collection, Public Conveniences, and Street Cleansing. We would then place documents and records connected with these specific areas within the folders, or we could further define the folder structure by creating additional folders within each of these areas. For example, under the Health and Safety folder, we would create another folder called Health and Safety Accidents and place documents such as, for example, the Health and Safety form — Report of an injury or dangerous occurrence (see Figure 4.4) that we have been using within the Health and Safety Accidents folder. Figure 5.1 illustrates an example of a folder structure based on the organizational structure.

Property-Based Folder Structures

Departments whose work involves dealing with properties, such as planning or building control, would normally file their paper-based records

Figure 5.1 Organizational folder structure.

and documents against property references connected to the addresses they deal with. The property-based approach to filing works well for departments whose primary business interest is property because it closely mimics the method they use to store paper-based documents and records.

With the property-based folder structure, the top-level folder would be name of the organization and is a container for all other folders in the document repository. The folders underneath the top-level folder would be those relating to property references. For example, the address — 100 High Street, Toon Town, Toon City, 10000 — may have a unique property reference number of 100001 assigned to it; thus, the property folder may be described as "100001 100 High Street 10000". Here we have used the unique property reference number, the first line of the address, and the zip code in creating a unique folder name to describe the property. Underneath each property folder you would create folders that describe each of the departments within the organization, i.e., Environmental Services, Planning Services, Building Control, etc. Underneath each of these folders you would create further folders to describe each team within the department, such as was undertaken for document groups, as illustrated in Chapter 4, Figure 4.2. Hence, underneath the Environmental Services folder you would create the following folders of Food, Health and Safety, Pest Control, Pollution, Recycling, Refuse Collection, Public Conveniences, and Street Cleansing. Furthermore, underneath each of the folders describing the document groups or teams, you can create further folders to describe the document types; i.e., for Health and Safety, these would be Accidents, Applications, Letters, Notices, Reports, and Contracts, as shown in Figure 4.3.

The sample document that we have been working with could then be placed underneath the Accidents folder. Alternatively, you can further define the folder structure by creating another folder underneath the Accidents folder, which may be labeled "ACME Corporation — John Smith — December 1, 2006," which would then enable you to file all correspondence relating to this one incident under this folder.

The property-based folder structure works very well for departments or teams who either work with properties such as Planning Services or Building Control and also for departments or teams who have historically filed their paperwork under property references. However, this folder structure does not work at all for teams who do not file their documents and records against properties. Using our example of the document groups defined in Figure 4.2, Street Cleansing documents and records could not be filed against properties or certain types of pollution such as Air Pollution. Figure 5.2 illustrates an example of a property-based folder structure.

Business-Based Folder Structure

The business-based folder structure would be suitable for departments that deal with other businesses and organizations, such as in our example of the health and safety department within Environmental Services, which commonly deals with other environmental agencies on a national level. The business-based folder structure would allow the department to group together all documents relating to a specific business or organization.

Under the business-based folder structure, documents and records can be further grouped together depending on the specific topic or incident. Taking our example of the Health and Safety form — report of an injury or dangerous occurrence, shown in Figure 4.4, using the business-based folder structure, we would create a folder called "XYZ Corporation." Under the folder "XYZ Corporation," we would then create another folder called "Health and Safety Accidents," and place this document under this folder. Alternatively, we could create another folder underneath "Health and Safety Accidents" called "John Smith," as well as attaching the date to the folder and then placing the actual document within this folder. This would mean effectively creating a new folder for every separate Health and Safety incident that has occurred relating to ACME Corporation. Figure 5.3 illustrates an example of organizing documents and records under the business-based folder structure.

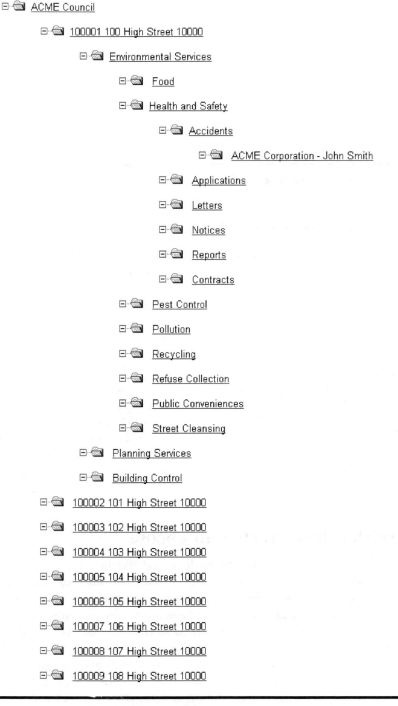

Figure 5.2 **Property-based folder structure.**

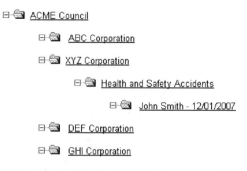

Figure 5.3 Business-based folder.

Project-Based Folder Structure

The project-based folder structure works well for organizations, and departments within an organization, whose work is primarily project based, as it can also encourage project teams to share the same workspace regardless of which department or team they are based in.

Using this approach, we would again create the top-level folder in the name of the organization, which becomes the container for all other folders. Folders at the second level would represent the projects within the organization, and hence would be named after the project names. Figure 5.4 illustrates an example of a project-based folder structure.

The advantages of a project-based folder structure is that it allows an organization that primarily works on projects to organize all documents and records on a project basis irrespective of the organizational structure, business name, or property structure. The disadvantage of this approach is that it tends to be only suitable for project-based work and not for non-project-based work.

Which Folder Structure to Choose

Each of the four folder structures discussed has its own advantages and disadvantages, with one being more flexible than another. The organizational folder structure is the most universal, easily mapping on to the existing organizational structure in terms of teams and departments, allowing the various sections of the organization to store their document and records within their corresponding sections. Hence, this folder structure would suit the vast majority of documents and records classification requirements.

The other folder structures, business-based, property-based, and project-based, are more suitable than the organizational-based folder structure for

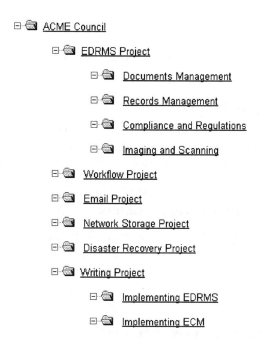

Figure 5.4   Project-based folder structure.

certain types of departments or teams. Thus, the questions remains: Which folder structure to go for?

The Hybrid Approach

Adopting an approach to creating the folder structure using a combination of all the four folder structures described previously — hence a *hybrid approach* — allows an organization to take advantage of the best folder structure depending on the needs and requirements of the individual team or section of the organization that you are creating it for.

As mentioned earlier in this book, and will be many times again, an effective and properly implemented EDRMS solution starts and ends with the people who will be using the system on a daily basis, i.e., the users within the organization. Therefore, it proves advantageous if we can create the folder structure in such a way that suits the needs of each individual team within the organizations. Hence, some teams would require a project-based folder structure, whereas others would prefer the business-based folder structure, and yet others would be happy to use the organizational-based folder structure.

The steps outlined in the following text illustrate how to create a folder structure for the Environmental Services department's teams and the Planning department using the hybrid approach.

Step 1 — Top-Level Folder

It is good practice, when creating any folder structure, to create a top-level folder that represents the organization, being labeled with the organization's name, and which will also be the container for all other folders.

Step 2 — Creating Level 2 Folders

These folders would exist directly underneath the top-level folders and would represent sections within the organization. In keeping with our previous examples, there would be Environmental Services, Planning Services, and Building Services.

Step 3 — Creating Level 3 Folders

These folders would represent each of the individual departments within the level 2 folder. For Environmental Services, these folders created should map directly on to the document groups, as defined in the previous chapter and shown in Figure 4.2.

For the Planning Services department, we would create property-based folders, i.e., each folder would represent a property, and the documents and records relating to those properties would be located within their respective property folder.

Step 4 — Creating Folders within Each of the Environmental Services Department Folders

So far, creating the folder structure has been straightforward because the structure simply maps on to the organization structure in terms of sections of the organizations and departments. Now we have to decide how to further group documents and records in the best possible way. Take, for example, the Health and Safety form — report of an injury or dangerous occurrence, as shown in Figure 4.4.

The question we need to consider is: Do we group all these documents together under a level 4 folder called Health and Safety Accidents, or do we attach this document to a level 4 folder that describes the organization where the incident occurred, or do we attach this document to a folder with a property reference?

There are now three different approaches that we can take in organizing documents and records within the health and safety folder.

First, we can follow the organizational folder structure and create a level 4 folder called Health and Safety Accidents, and place all documents and records relating to health and safety accidents, injuries, and dangerous occurrences under this folder.

Second, we can follow the business-based folder structure and create a folder that is named after the organization, and place all documents and records relating to the organization in this folder. Finally, we can follow the property-based folder structure and create a folder that describes the property on which this incident occurred.

The correct approach to take depends upon how the team wishes to store its documents and records, as well as which folder structure will be easiest to maintain in the long run. An illustrated example of the hybrid approach to defining the folder structure is shown in Figure 5.5.

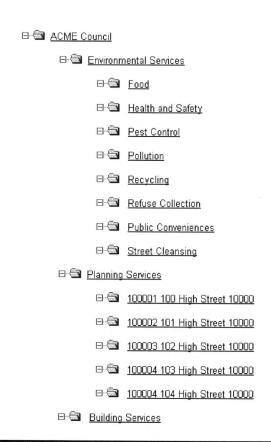

Figure 5.5   Hybrid folder structure.

Chapter 6

Search and Retrieval

The ability to adequately search for and retrieve documents and records is just as important as classifying and indexing documents and records. Classifying and indexing documents and records can be considered as one half of the EDRMS coin, whereas searching for documents and records and retrieving them is the other half.

In Chapter 4, "Creating Electronic Document Types," we discussed the importance of classifying and indexing documents in the correct and proper manner to facilitate easy and efficient searching and retrieval of documents. In this chapter we discuss the different approaches to searching for and retrieving documents as well as presenting a step-by-step approach to designing search screens for the electronic document types we have already created.

Searching a Document or Records Content

Being able to search the text content of a document or record is one of the most useful search functions an EDRMS solution can have. To be able to search the text content of a historic record that has been scanned into the system from a paper source, the document or record will have to undergo OCR (Optical Character Recognition) either at the moment it is scanned and indexed or at a later time.

An OCR function recognizes words on a typed document and indexes these words, enabling search mechanisms to search for both individual words and phrases within a document. For example, if a user wanted to find all documents relating to the accident of John Smith at the ACME Corporation but did not know how these documents or records were classified or indexed, then, if the document or record they were searching for had undergone OCR indexing, the user would be able to locate all document and records containing the words "John Smith ACME Corporation" using the OCR search facility.

The search field used for searching a document or records content may be labeled "Keywords" or "Document Content," and upon the user typing in the words "John Smith ACME Corporation," the search would then return all the documents and records containing any of the words typed into the search field.

It is also important to give users the flexibility to choose how the search facility searches the content of a document or record, especially when designing advanced search screens. Basic search screens do not need this level of configuration within the search facility because most users would want to type in a couple of words, hit return, and view a list of documents or records within a couple of seconds.

With advanced search screens, if a user were to type in the words "John Smith ACME Corporation," then they should also be able to select how the search facility treats those words. The user could then select that the search facility list all documents containing any one of those words, all of those words, or the exact phrase. The user may also want to specify two separate phrases of "John Smith" and "ACME Corporation" and then specify whether the search were to return documents with either one of the phrases, e.g., "John Smith" OR "ACME Corporation," or both of those phrases, e.g., "John Smith" AND "ACME Corporation."

Basic Searches

Basic search screens should allow the user to search for a particular document type or search across all document types. The user should be able to select either all document types or a particular document type from a drop-down list of document types. As well as allowing the user to select a particular document, the search screen should also allow the user to search the documents content by allowing the user to type in words into a search field labeled document content. The basic search mechanism should then look for any of the words contained within the document or records content that match the document type selected, or any document or record if a document type has not been specified.

The idea with a basic search is to offer the user a search facility that is as basic as possible but that also helps them to quickly and easily find the documents or records they are looking for. An example of a basic search screen is shown in Figure 6.1.

The basic search can also be slightly enhanced by allowing the users to specify the way in which they wish to search the documents' content. An option to search for "any of the words," "all of the words," or "exact phrase" could be offered to the user for searching the documents' content; however, as this is a basic search screen, the default for document content searching should be search for "any of the words." Offering these options in a simple drop-down list will allow users to select the exact option they want. An example of this type of basic search screen is shown in Figure 6.2.

The advantage of designing the basic search screen as described in Figure 6.2 is that it allows the user greater flexibility in specifying the search criteria for the documents' content. For example, if a user wanted to search for documents or records concerning "John Smith" and "ACME Corporation," then a user with slightly more know-how concerning searching could select the "exact phrase" option for searching the document or records content, effectively specifying the value of *"John Smith" AND "ACME Corporation,"* which will result in the search returning only those documents that contained both phrases. Hence, fewer document or records

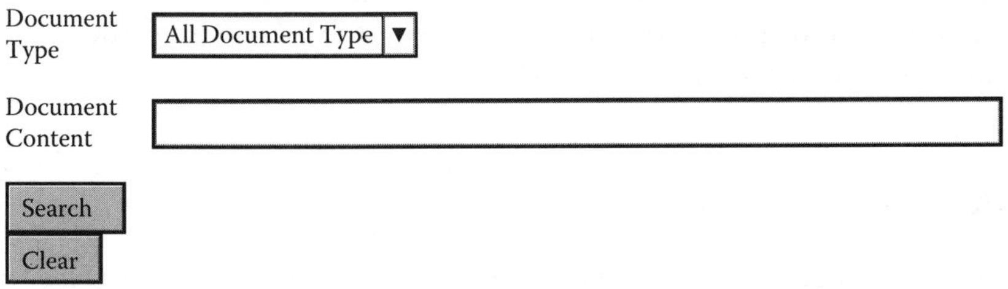

Figure 6.1 Basic search screen.

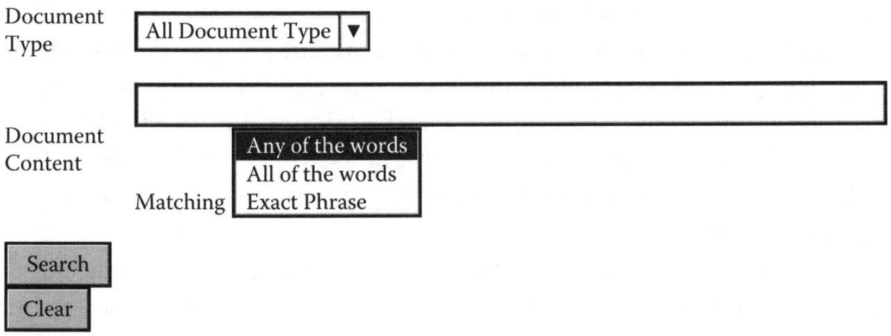

Figure 6.2 Basic search screen with selection for how to search document content.

would be returned, allowing users to easily find the document or record they require in much less time because they would not have to sift through as many documents as they would have had to if the "exact phrase" option was not selected.

If the basic search screen was offered to the users as specified in Figure 6.1, they would not have any control over the basic search, would search for document content, and all documents containing any of the words for "John Smith ACME Corporation" would be returned. There could literally be hundreds of documents or records in the documents repository that matched any of the words "John Smith ACME Corporation." This would mean that it would take users much longer to find the document or record they are looking for because they would be sifting through hundreds of documents or records compared to say tens of documents if they were able to specify the "exact phrase," as in Figure 6.2.

Once again, it must be stressed that because we are designing a basic search screen for novice users, we have to offer them the simplest of searches, which means defaulting searching for both any document type and searching document content for any of the words.

It has been said many times before throughout this book that the type of basic search you choose to implement will depend upon the individual organization and, more specifically, the way the staff within the organization cope with the change to EDRMS.

Advanced Searches

Advanced searches should offer the user the ultimate flexibility in allowing users to specify search criteria to exactly match the documents and records they are attempting to search. The Advanced Search screen should offer different search criteria fields depending on the document type you are searching for with the search criteria fields mirroring the metadata fields specified for the document type. For example, an advanced search screen for the Health and Safety document — report of an injury or dangerous occurrence will have the same search criteria fields shown on an Advanced Search screen for this document as shown in Chapter 4, Figure 4.9, titled "Complete metadata definitions for the Health and Safety Accident document."

Advanced Search screens should also allow the user to specify the date ranges of documents they want the search to return. For example, if a user wanted to find all health and safety — report of an injury or dangerous occurrence documents filed between May 1 and December 1, 2006, then the advanced search screen should allow the user to specify a start date of May 1, 2006, and an end date of December 1, 2006. The advanced search will then work on the date range of May 1, 2006, and December 1, 2006, and any other search criteria that may or may not have been specified, and return only those documents within this particular date range. Allowing users to specify a date range allows for much more accurate searching and retrieval of documents because the number of documents returned would be smaller than if they were not able to specify a date range.

An advanced search for any document type should allow the user to build up Boolean expressions using AND/OR. For example, if a user wanted to search for all health and safety reports of a dangerous occurrence document and records for "John Smith," "ACME Corporation," between the dates of "May 1, 2006" and "December 1, 2006," then, in constructing this search criteria, the option should be given to search for documents containing both the phrases "John Smith" AND "ACME Corporation," or either one of the phrases "John Smith" OR "ACME Corporation" within the date range specified.

The search for "John Smith" AND "ACME Corporation" would result in a less number of documents and records being returned by the search. However, if after this search returned its results and if users did not find the documents or records they were looking for, they could then opt to rerun the search using OR instead of AND, thus instructing the search to locate documents and records that contain either one of the phrases "John Smith" OR "ACME Corporation" between the date range specified. This would then return more documents and records than the previous search that specified "John Smith" OR "ACME Corporation."

Designing Search Screens and Displaying Search Results

It is important to design all search screens so that they are as intuitive and as easy to use as possible; this will greatly help users in the organization to get to grips with the new EDRMS solution. If the search screens are not easy and intuitive to use, or there is no basic search facility or facility to search a document's or record's content, then this will be a significant hindrance for users because they will find it difficult to locate documents and records within the system. The effect of having unsatisfied users could ultimately lead to the system failing; hence the importance of designing easy-to-use, initiative search screens.

We have already covered the designing basic search screens as illustrated in Figure 6.1 and Figure 6.2; however, we have not discussed how documents or records lists should be displayed after the search has been performed, or the design of advanced search screens.

After hitting the search button on any search page, whether it is a basic search or an advanced search, documents and records matching the search criteria should be displayed in a tabular format on the screen. The search results page should indicate the total amount of records found, e.g., 455 documents and records found, and should also display a set number of documents or records per page. The number of documents or records displayed per page can be set to a default figure of 25; however, the user should also be able to specify the number of documents or records they want returned on the page by selecting from predetermined values such as 10, 25, 50, and 100 documents or records per page. In the case of 455 documents or records being returned, the user should be able to move back and forth from page to page, paging through search results much like how an Internet search engine displays results.

In order to make the individual search results easier to view, the search page should display these results in alternating colors. Any colors will do; however, grey and white work well and generally offer a neutral, if not somewhat bland, approach to displaying lists of search results such as documents and records.

Important information to display per search result is the title of the document or record, the date the document or record has on it, the date it was last modified, and the file size in kilobytes (Kb). Descriptions for these heading fields can be shortened to Title, Document Date, Modified Date, and Size (Kb), respectively.

Users should also have the option of being able to sort the search results list by clicking on any one of the field headings. For example, if they wanted to sort a list of search results by title, by simply clicking on document title, the page should then sort the documents by title into ascending order, A–Z. If the documents are already in ascending order, clicking on the title field header should reverse the order the documents or records are displayed in, thus displaying them in descending order, Z–A. The same would apply to the document date field header and other field header used to display the results of a search. An example of a page displaying a list of search results in shown in Figure 6.3.

With regard to designing advanced search screens, the actual search fields shown on the screen will depend on the metadata that has been defined for the document type. As mentioned in the previous section on advanced searches, the search fields should be an exact representation of the metadata fields defined for the document type.

From a technical point of view, the advanced search screen needs to be able to read in the metadata associated with the document type that has been selected and then display the required search fields. Both start date and end date search fields should be displayed, allowing the user to specify a date range for documents and records returned by the search.

Search Results for "Any Document Type" Containing any of the words
"Project Requirements"

Displaying 11–20 of 255
documents/records

Display [10] [▼]
documents/records per page

Title	Document Date	Modified Date	Size (Kb)
Functional Specification for EDRMS Project	01/16/2007	02/18/2007	52
Technical Specification for EDRMS Project	01/30/2007	02/28/2007	64
EDRMS Compliance and Regulations	01/10/2006	01/10/2006	120
Network Storage Project Initiation Document	05/12/2006	06/15/2006	255
Workflow Project Requirements	01/12/2005	02/05/2006	125
Disaster Recovery Requirements Project	05/06/2005	05/06/2005	55
Information Systems Requirements Project	07/06/2005	12/06/2005	451
EDRMS Searching Requirements	01/05/2005	08/05/2005	85
EDRMS Hardware Requirements	04/07/2005	15/07/2005	79
Email Project Requirements	01/14/2006	01/28/2005	31

Prev 1 2 3 4 5 6 7 8 9 10 Next

Figure 6.3 List of search results.

The advanced search should allow the user to build search criteria in to a Boolean expression, allowing the user to select either AND/OR after specifying search values in any fields except the date range fields. This will allow the user to build up Boolean expressions specifying that documents or records must contain certain words and/or phrases as discussed using the examples of "John Smith" and "ACME Corporation" previously.

With regards to dates, if a user has specified a start date without an end date, then the search should locate all documents or records that have a document date that is either the same as the start date that has been specified or have a document date that is after the document has been created. The reverse is true for specifying an end date without a start date — all documents or records that are dated up to and including the end date specified should be returned. An example of the advanced search screen for the Health and Safety document — report of an injury or dangerous occurrence is shown in Figure 6.4.

Health and Safety - Report of an injury or dangerous occurrence		
Reporting Person's Surname		AND ▼
Reporting Person's Forename		AND ▼
Reporting Person's Initials		AND ▼
Job Title		AND ▼
Telephone Number		AND ▼
Organization Name		AND ▼
Organization Address		AND ▼
Organization Postcode		AND ▼
Organization Business Type		AND ▼
Incident Date		AND ▼
Incident Time		AND ▼
Incident Location (Department/Premises)		AND ▼
Did the incident occur at the address mentioned above	☐	
Elsewhere in your organization	☐	
At someone else's premises	☐	
A public place	☐	
Incident Address and Postcode		AND ▼
Incident Local Authority		AND ▼
Reporting Party Surname		AND ▼
Reporting Party Forename		AND ▼
Reporting Party Initials		AND ▼
Injured Person's Address		AND ▼
Injured Person's Postcode		AND ▼
Injured Person's Sex	▼	AND ▼
Injury Type	▼	AND ▼
Injured Person's Condition		
	☐ Become Unconscious	AND ▼
	☐ Need resuscitation	AND ▼
	☐ Remain in hospital for more than 24 hours	AND ▼
	☐ None of the above	AND ▼
Type of Accident	Contact with moving machinery or material being machined ▼	AND ▼
Start Date		AND ▼
End Date		AND ▼
Matching	Any of the word ▼	AND ▼
Document Content		
Search Clear		

Figure 6.4   Advanced search screen for the Health and Safety document — report of an injury or dangerous occurrence.

Administrative Search Functions — Reporting

Administrative search functions can help both system administrators as well as persons responsible for development and implementation of the EDRMS solution by providing useful information about how users are using the search functions to locate documents and records.

This can be achieved by building in search reporting functionality available only to administrative users of the system. The search reporting functionality should provide detailed analysis of how users have searched for documents and records over varying time periods. These predefined reports should be offered for both basic searches and advanced searches separately.

Reporting facilities for basic searches should include options for the administrative user to view all searches carried out over specific set time periods as well as reporting by grouping document types together. Time periods should include all searches carried out today, last week, last month, and last year, as well as offering administrative users the ability to enter and run reports using their own date range.

In order to achieve this search reporting functionality, there needs be a background process that logs all searches and search results, so that these can be queried and reported on at a later date. The search report should include the date and time the search was performed, the keywords that were entered, such as "ACME Corporation," the user or user ID of the person who carried out the search, the search type option chosen, such as "Contains all words" or "Contains any words," and the number of search results returned as well as totals for amount of searches carried out for the time period.

Such reports can help administrators to find out how users are using the search functionality in the system, how frequently they are using the searches, and which are the most popular search options.

This ultimately helps the systems designers and implementers to improve searching and retrieval mechanisms. Figure 6.5 displays an example search-reporting page, showing the options for basic search and advance search–search reports, and Figure 6.6 displays an example search report for the basic search.

The same type of consideration also needs to be given to advanced search reports. However, because of the nature of advanced search screens having different search fields depending on the document type being searched, the advanced search report will be displayed in a slightly different manner.

Search Reports

Basic Search

- Today
- Yesterday
- Last Week
- Last Month
- Last Year
- From these dates

Advanced Search

- Today
- Yesterday
- Last Week
- Last Month
- Last Year
- From these dates

Figure 6.5   Basic search and advanced search reporting page.

As with the basic search reports, document types should be grouped, and the reports should contain the user or user ID of the person who carried out the search, the document content search type chosen, the number of search results returned, as well as the totals for amount of searches carried out for the time period selected. The reporting time periods should be the same as that offered for basic search reports, such as today, last week, last month, and last year, as well as allowing administrative users the ability to enter their own date range. It is with regard to displaying search criteria for the advanced search reports that the report differs from a basic search report. Here we will have to summarize the search criteria entered and then display this in the advanced search report. Summarizing the search criteria can often use up to 15 lines in the report; therefore, it is very useful to have a facility that expands and collapses the search criteria in order to save space. An example advanced search report is shown in Figure 6.7.

Basic Search - Search Report for 01/20/2007 - 01/20/2007

Generated on 01/20/2007 11:25:53

Date and Time	User ID	Document Type	Search Type	Keywords	Number of Results
01/20/2007 08:31:45	9675 - John Smith	All Document Types	Any of the words	Information Systems	55
01/20/2007 09:34:58	2035 - Mary Jo	All Document Types	Any of the words	EDRMS Project	15
01/20/2007 09:35:09	2035 - Mary Jo	All Document Types	Any of the words	John Smith	83
01/20/2007 10:18:14	4550 - Alex Smith	All Document Types	All of the words	ACME Corporation	47
01/20/2007 10:29:52	8550 - John Dee	IT Document Type	Exact phrase	Proprietary Scanning Systems	5
01/20/2007 10:33:14	8550 - John Dee	All Document Types	Any of the words	Storage Network	75
01/20/2007 10:38:47	1225 - Jack James	All Document Types	Any of the words	Email	89
01/20/2007 10:45:32	5500 - Fred Roberts	IT Document Type	Exact phrase	Email Storage	7
01/20/2007 10:49:11	4125 - Angela Right	All Document Types	Any of the words	Sales Forecasts	125
01/20/2007 10:55:51	6350 - Jessie Wong	All Document Types	Any of the words	Computer Projects	450
01/20/2007 10:59:02	6330 - Kevin Adams	All Document Types	Any of the words	Marketing Ideas	74
01/20/2007 11:09:36	6880 - Ian Quick	IT Document Type	Exact phrase	C++ Programming Reference	6
01/20/2007 11:17:23	9655 - Sam Harper	Corporate Document Type	Exact phrase	EDRMS Project Feasibility Study	1
01/20/2007 11:19:52	8450 - Fredrick Harp	All Document Types	All of the words	Network Projects	84
01/20/2007 11:21:54	4125 - Angela Right	All Document Types	All of the words	Email Projects	152
01/20/2007 11:23:11	2225 - Fred James	All Document Types	Any of the words	Telephone Systems	147
01/20/2007 11:24:39	2225 - Fred James	All Document Types	Any of the words	Security Systems Analysis	251

Figure 6.6   Search report for the basic search.

Advanced Search - Search Report for 01/20/2007 - 01/20/2007
Generated on 01/20/2007 15:30:30

Date and Time	User ID	Document Type	Search Type	Search Criteria	Keywords	Number of Results
01/20/2007 09:25:05	9675 - J. Smith	IT Document Type	Any of the words	+ *Click to view*	Information systems	10
01/20/2007 09:25:05	4450 - A. Smith	Health and Safety Accident	Any of the words	+ *Click to view*	ACME Corporation John Smith	14
01/20/2007 09:25:05	8550 - J. Dee	Pest Control	Any of the words	+ *Click to view*	Large Rodents	5
01/20/2007 09:25:05	5500 - F. Roberts	IT Document Type	Exact Phrase	+ *Click to view*	Network Storage Project	8
01/20/2007 09:25:05	8450 - F. Harp	Street Cleansing	All of the words	+ *Click to view*	105 High Street 10000	4
01/20/2007 09:25:05	6350 - J. Wong	Food	Any of the words	+ *Click to view*	ACME Takeaways	3
01/20/2007 09:25:05	4125 - A. Right	Planning Services	All of the words	+ *Click to view*	100 High Street 10000	2
01/20/2007 09:25:05	6330 - K. Adams	Recycling	Exact Phrase	+ *Click to view*	Bio-degradable recycling project	7
01/20/2007 09:25:05	2225 - F. James	Building Services	Any of the words	+ *Click to view*	Structural defects in 1930s apartments	6

Figure 6.7   Search report for the advanced search.

Chapter 7

Integrating Workflow

Workflow, also known as Business Process Management (BPM), allows an organization to route electronic documents around the organization to different departments and individuals depending on the particular work-related tasks that need to be undertaken concerning that document.

The vast majority of documents flow around an organization, passing from one individual to another, and also passing from one department to another. For example, letters received in the post arrive in the post room and, in the post room, the letters are sorted into their relevant departments and then distributed to those departments, teams, and individuals. When the letters arrive on an individual's desk, depending on the type of action needed, they may be logged on to the system and another letter written in response, or they could be passed onto another department or team to be acted upon.

This flow of letters within the organization is known as the letters' workflow, which can be handled manually by individuals physically taking the documents from one room to another room, or it can be handled electronically using workflow. This chapter is concerned with integrating workflow with electronic documents and presents a stepped approach to integrating workflow into the EDRM system.

How and When Should Workflow Be Integrated?

We can take two different approaches to integrating workflow. Workflow can be implemented after the main EDRMS solution has been implemented and can build upon the existing document or records functionality, or workflow can be implemented in parallel with the implementation of the EDRMS solution.

There are pros and cons to both these different approaches. However, the most determining factor should be how the users, i.e., the staff in the organization, would react and cope with the implementation of EDRMS.

If it is determined by the project leaders that staff across the organization would cope well with the change to EDRMS, then consideration could be given to implementing workflow in parallel with the EDRMS implementation. If, on the other hand, the cultural change regarding EDRMS were initially presenting difficulties to the staff by way of resistance to the new system, then it would probably be best to implement the workflow component of the system at a later date after the main EDRM system has been implemented successfully.

The decision as whether to implement both EDRM and workflow together or implement workflow after the main EDRMS implementation really depends on the organization and its staff. As previously mentioned, a successful implementation of EDRMS begins and ends with the users on site.

Workflow Process Mapping

Workflow process mapping is used to define and map out diagrammatically the way in which a given document travels around an organization. The method involves first investigating how documents travel around the organization, and then representing this flow as individual tasks and stages on a diagram. Workflow process mapping is the method we will be using to integrate workflow with electronic documents in this chapter. In order to begin the process of workflow process mapping, we first need to investigate how documents flow around the organization, starting at the beginning of that flow, looking at where documents come into the organization.

Starting at the Beginning — The Post Room

The vast majority of documents come into an organization via traditional mail services, i.e., surface and airmail post, and get delivered to the post room in most medium and large organizations. It is therefore important to start our workflow processes from the post room.

The scanning and indexing operations within the post room would involve opening all mail and scanning the mail in batches, and then briefly indexing the mail at scanning and indexing stations before selecting the department, team, or individual that the mail is addressed to. This approach to handling mail would involve quite a significant cultural change to most organizations, namely, that mail would be scanned and indexed at scanning stations as opposed to being physically sorted into batches and delivered to individual rooms. This cultural change is discussed in greater detail in Chapter 20, "Managing the Cultural Change of EDRMS." However, if workflow is to be integrated, it is important to integrate it throughout the whole life cycle of a document.

Setting Up the Post Room

Setting up the post room in order to handle mail electronically means redesigning the method in which mail is handled. Traditionally, mail would have been handled in a fashion whereby sacks of post come into the post room and are sorted by hand into batches by department and/or room number. Once sorted by departments and/or room numbers, the mail would then be physically taken to each department or room and given to either a clerical member of the staff to distribute to individuals or may be handed to the individuals directly. Using an electronic workflow-based solution in delivering mail would significantly reduce the need to physically deliver mail because mail would appear in users' work queues.

The following text outlines a stepped approach that can be taken to discover how many scanning stations and staff are required for your organization's post room.

Step 1 — How Much Mail Does the Organization Receive?

The first task in implementing workflow is to find out how many individual items of mail your organization receives on a daily basis. In working out the average daily number of individual items of mail received, it is important to factor in issues such as busy times of the year. For example, an accounting practice may receive extremely high volumes of mail the month before tax returns are due in. Therefore, it is important to set aside capacity, both in terms of human resources and computer systems' resources, to cope with any elevated levels of demand for post room scanning and indexing tasks.

To work out the average daily number of individual items of mail the organization receives, it is best to choose an average time of year when the organization is neither experiencing low levels nor high levels of mail.

The mail should be counted on a daily basis for a period of about two weeks or a month. Parcels and direct marketing mail (junk mail) should not be included in the count of individual items of mail but should instead be counted separately. After this time period during which the mail has been counted has elapsed, the mean averages can be worked out by dividing the total individual items of mail for the entire period by the number of days the mail was counted. You should now have two averages for mail coming in to your organization — one average for the individual items of mail, i.e., envelopes and the like, and another for parcels and direct marketing mail, i.e., junk mail.

Now that we have these averages, we can use them to work out how many scanning stations and staff members will be needed to scan and index the mail each day.

Step 2 — How Do We Index Mail?

The initial indexing of mail in the post room should be a straightforward task, as at this stage there is no need for complex, in-depth indexing. The classification of mail, i.e., classifying a document as a particular document type, and indexing, i.e., assigning values to the document type's metadata fields, should be left to the user receiving the mail document.

Indexing letters in the post room should consist of the date the letter was received and specifying the department, team, or individual that the letter is addressed to in order to route it to them. To speed up the indexing process, the date should be automatically generated for all letters that are indexed, thereby saving time and keystrokes for the staff indexing the letters. Regarding specifying the department, team, or individual, these selections should be available via drop-down list boxes, again speeding up the indexing process and also reducing the risk of human typing errors. An example letter indexing form is shown in Figure 7.1, which also corresponds to the metadata definitions for the letter document type defined in Chapter 4 and shown in Figure 4.10, with the addition of two extra metadata fields to select department and individual.

Step 3 — How Many Scanning and Indexing Stations Are Needed?

In order to find out how long it will take to scan and index the post received by an organization on an average day, a number of dry runs using a test system would have to be carried out. You will have to allow for staff training factors as well, e.g., clerical staff will automatically perform the tasks of scanning and indexing the post in a more efficient and faster manner after they have had time to get used to the system.

Department	Administrative Support Department ▼
Individual	John Smith ▼

From Forename	
From Surname	
From Company	
Your Ref	
Our Ref	
Description	
Date	

Figure 7.1 Letter indexing form.

Using dry runs on a test system will enable you to work out how many scanning stations are needed. For example, if 1000 individual items of mail are received per day, and it takes 5 hr for one person to scan and index these items, then it can be ascertained that approximately 200 items can be scanned and indexed per hour. Thus, assuming that the mail arrives at 9 am, for everybody in the organization to receive their mail by 12 noon, it would require two scanning stations with two members of staff scanning and indexing at the very least. In this scenario, three scanning stations and three members of staff scanning and indexing would be a better solution because then the job could be comfortably completed in 2 hr well before the 12 noon deadline for receiving mail.

Using this scenario, another option to consider would be having just one scanning station and two indexing stations. Most medium-sized scanners are able to scan at least 50 sheets per minute, so there could be one person opening letters, removing staples, and scanning the letters in, making sure they have been scanned properly, and then these batches of letters could be indexed by another two people at separate dedicated indexing stations. As indexing generally takes a longer time than scanning, it is advantageous to have more than one person indexing.

There is also the need to factor in spare capacity in the equation both in terms of human resources and spare computer resources because scanners and computers do break down, as well as staff taking days off due to sickness or annual leave. Hence, such events can have a major impact on the organization's ability to deliver mail, causing a knock-on effect throughout the rest of the organization.

In the scenario just described, with either three scanning and indexing stations or one scanning station and two indexing stations, there would be a need for an additional scanning and indexing station, which could operate both as a separate scanning station or a separate indexing station, depending on the mailroom scanning and indexing setup. There is also a need to have spare administrative staff on hand who have been trained to both scan and index mail and are able to do so in a proficient manner whenever the needs arises.

What Do We Do with Direct Marketing Materials?

So far we have talked about letters as individual items of mail. However, a significant percentage of an organization's mail, especially to certain departments such as Information Technology, consists of direct-marketing materials, commonly referred to as junk mail, catalogues, or brochures.

Direct-marketing materials such as brochures and catalogues cannot easily be scanned and indexed, and will therefore need to be handled in the same manual fashion as before, i.e., being physically delivered to departments and individuals. As direct-marketing materials do not constitute any part of the organization's business records, they do not need be integrated into an EDRM system or have workflow processes attached to them because they can simply be delivered to the recipients' desks without any further action being taken.

The Starting Point for Documents with Workflow

Given the foregoing example, all documents that are delivered to the organization received in the post will start life as simple letter documents as far as the EDRM and workflow systems are concerned. Only after these documents have been sent to the departments and individuals responsible for taking action on them will they need to be reclassified by their actual electronic document type. For example, a health and safety document — report of an injury or dangerous occurrence may get delivered to the post room, and only when it has been sent to the health and safety department is it reclassified from a letter document type to a health and safety accident document type and then be stored in the EDRM document repository accordingly.

Documents and forms that are delivered via fax or electronic mail can be classified and stored in the EDRM document repository as their actual document types right from start and can also drop in to the workflow process stage skipping the post room stage because these documents or forms have not come into the organization via the post room.

Work Queues

Letters that have previously been scanned and indexed by the post room would be received into the users' work queues. The staff in the organization would have their own individual work queues containing all their currently active tasks, including letters. A user's individual work queue is very similar to an e-mail applications inbox; however, instead of receiving e-mails as an e-mail applications inbox would, the work queue consists of job requests that documents can be attached to.

Handling Letters That Have Been Directed to the Wrong Department or Person

There will be occasions when letters have been scanned in by the post room but incorrectly indexed and sent to the wrong person or department. To handle this event, the letter workflow needs to allow the recipient of the letter (in this case the person or department to whom the letter has been sent) the ability to reassign the letter to another person or department.

In designing the workflow for the letter document type, the ability to reassign letters to different people and departments at any time needs to be taken into consideration. An example workflow for letters is shown in Figure 7.2.

Archiving Letters

In certain cases, no further action will be taken for certain letters; however, you may wish to retain the letters for specific periods of time. For example, a supplier may be informing a staff member about a new product or service they are launching, and although the organization is not under any legislative obligation to retain the letter, the staff member may wish to retain the letter for his or her own future reference. Thus, the workflow system needs to interface with the EDRMS solution to facilitate the retention of letters for specific periods of time.

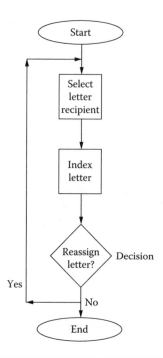

Figure 7.2   Letter workflow.

Investigating How Documents Flow around the Organization

To create a workflow process map for a given document, we first need to investigate how that document travels around the organization. This can be achieved by working with an individual who currently uses the document in his or her day-to-day tasks. Let's take, for example, the Health and Safety document — Report of an injury or dangerous occurrence that we have been working with in previous chapters.

This form would normally be received either via e-mail, fax, or post, and would be directed to the health and safety department. The document would then be reviewed by a staff member who may take one of several actions after reviewing the document. Further action may include investigating the incident and writing a report, referring the incident to another agency such as the Health and Safety Executive, or referring the form to another person or their line manager, as well as informing other departments of the incident, such as the legal department or building department where necessary.

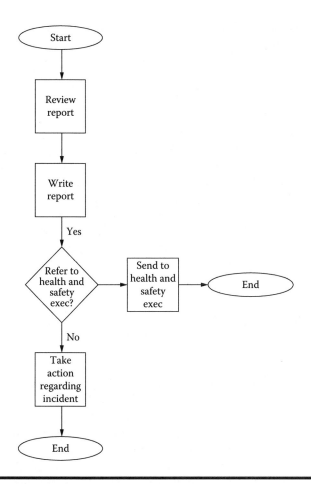

Figure 7.3 Health and Safety Accident workflow.

The possible flow of this document in terms of how the document passes from individuals or departments in the organization needs to be depicted on a workflow process map. An example workflow process map for this particular example is shown in Figure 7.3.

Keeping an Audit Trail

The importance of auditing and the ability to keep an audit trail has been mentioned previously in Chapter 2 in discussing the functionality of both EDM and ERM systems, and it is true for documents connected to workflow processes. Every time a document is subject to change, and every time a document gets passed from one user to another, in fact, every time there is an action on a particular document, this needs to be recorded by the system and logged.

An effective auditing process that records all actions performed on a document, whether that document may consist of an application, or whether that particular document may have a task associated with it that requires processing, will allow managers and other staff in the organization to see exactly what has happened to the document, effectively creating an audit trail for that document or case.

The advantages of an audit trail include accountability, e.g., you can see who has taken what action on which documents, cases, or applications, and at what time the action was taken. Another important advantage includes the ability for line managers to easily manage their staff's workloads, ensuring that documents or cases do not get lost in the system as they will reside in individual or departmental work queues, and their audit trails can be checked easily.

Running Reports

The ability to run reports on workflow processes and their associated documents is a very useful feature of a workflow system that is capable of providing statistical analysis to the organization. For example, someone in the organization may want to know how many planning applications have been received in the last month, and how long, on average, it has taken to process. Building in reporting facilities and designing a set of prebuilt reports to the workflow system allows information of this kind to be easily retrieved within a matter of minutes as opposed to manually counting documents and manually extracting the information contained within the documents.

Predesigned reports need to be attached to every workflow process, and access to query building functionality needs to be provided to allow administrative users of the system to design and run their own bespoke reports.

Managing the Organization Using Workflow

One very powerful aspect of workflow is the ability that line managers have in managing their staff's workload. A properly implemented workflow system that is integrated with an EDRMS solution would allow line managers to manage their staff's work queues by allowing them to view the individual work queues as well as assigning jobs to their staff via the latter's work queues.

In order for the workflow system to provide functionality around these line management tasks, the organizational structure would need to be represented in the workflow system. Looking at the organizational structure from a workflow-centric point of view would mean that the workflow system could define the organization's structure and could also be integrated with other systems such as human resources and personnel.

Representing the organizational structure in the workflow system would not just allow the line manager of a department to view his or her staff's work queues and assign jobs but also allow that line manager's manager to view that line manager's workload, and so on until we get to the top of the organizational tree. Hence, the chief executive would be able to view the work queues for everyone in the organization while assigning jobs and tasks to his directors or senior managers, who would assign tasks to their staff and so on down the organizational structure.

Using workflow allows the organization to incorporate business processes, documents, and people together into workflow processes, which means that the organization is now accountable because, every case, job, or task is tracked and audited, and can be reported upon.

Workflow can be considered as the glue that brings business processes, documents, and people together.

Other Workflow Examples

Any business process can be automated using a workflow approach, as mentioned previously. To develop a workflow, you need to investigate how the document travels around the organization. Job Applications and Freedom of Information Requests are just two of the possible applications for workflow.

Job Applications

Job Applications arrive in an organization in a variety of ways. They are received through the post, via the Internet, and via recruitment consultants, and hence come into the organization at different places. Job Applications in the recruitment process can also take on a number of different routes. Some will be discarded after the initial review of the application form, some will get shortlisted for interview, and others will receive a call for an interview. Some recruitment processes will require a second interview, references will be sought at a particular stage, and some applications will be successful with individuals receiving an offer of employment.

At each of these stages the recruitment process for a particular individual applicant can end. For successful applications, although the particular recruitment workflow process would have ended, other processes concerning the start of the employment contract need to occur, such as the individual's record being entered into a personnel or human resources system and all the associated tasks that occur at this stage. Hence, with successful applications, another workflow process or even multiple workflow processes can be started to accommodate the needs of human resources and other tasks connected with the employment of the new recruit, such as security access. Figure 7.4 illustrates the workflow process map for the Job Application workflow.

Freedom of Information Request

Figure 7.5 illustrates the workflow process map for the Freedom of Information Request workflow. In this workflow, a Freedom of Information (FOI) request comes in to the organization and gets assigned to a particular person. If the request can be satisfied, i.e., the information is deemed suitable to be released and is not of a sensitive nature, then it is sent to the customer of the FOI request. If, on the other hand, the information is deemed unsuitable to be released for whatever reason, then the information is not released; however, the customer is still informed about his or her FOI Request.

Realizing the Full Potential of Workflow

The power of workflow and business process management along with business process re-engineering, and the methods used to convert existing business processes into a more streamlined workflow approach, have the potential to streamline organizations, saving costs all round in terms of time, finances, and human resources needed to accomplish a vast majority of business tasks. However, because the implementation of workflow has the effect of saving the organization costs in terms of human resources, it can often be difficult to implement it in terms of getting the organization's staff to buy in because some staff members in the organization may feel that the "new computer system" is there to replace their jobs.

As mentioned earlier, getting the users on the side of the management in any implementation of workflow is an extremely important factor, one that cannot be overlooked. The users' reaction to the new system is critical to the successful implementation of any system. Chapter 18, "Managing the Cultural Change of EDRMS," goes into greater detail discussing how the implementation of the new system and the organizational cultural

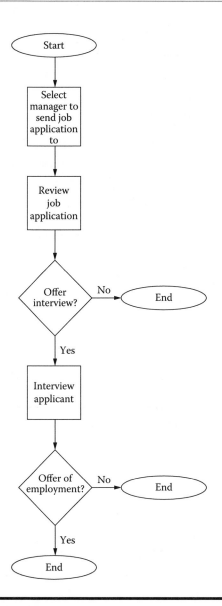

Figure 7.4 Job Application workflow.

change could be managed through the implementation of an effective change management program.

To sum up, workflow integrated with an EDRMS solution can radically improve an organization's efficiency as long as those who make up the organization — the staff — accept the solution and work with it, not against it.

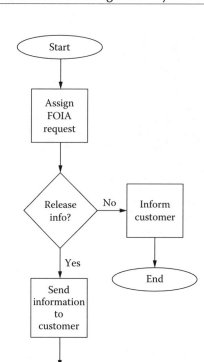

Figure 7.5   Freedom of Information Act (FOIA) request workflow.

Chapter 8

E-mail Management

E-mail is probably the most common means of communication both within organizations and across organizations today. Each time an e-mail is sent or received either within an organization or received from outside — from another organization or individual — a business record of the communication detailed in the e-mail has been made. As e-mails constitute business records, we need to define how we can manage these business records in terms of retaining e-mails so as to comply with standards and legislation governing an organization's documents and records.

Managing e-mails is a comprehensive topic, worthy of a book on its own. However, this chapter will discuss the fundamental aspects of e-mail management and how it fits into document and records management.

How to Manage E-mails

To manage e-mails, do we simply retain every single one that is both sent and received by the organization? In theory, this method could be used, but in practice it would be totally impractical. Simply imagine the amount of storage space required. For most medium- to large-size organizations, this would quickly run into terabytes (1024 Gigabytes) of data; hence, we need to define which e-mails need to be retained and which can be discarded. Essentially, the organization needs a set of rules defining its Corporate E-mail Policy and, within this policy, the rules for retaining e-mails need to be clearly defined.

Corporate E-mail Policy

The Corporate E-mail Policy should set out procedures that all staff in the organization must follow. It needs to explain what e-mail use is acceptable and what is not within the organization, and whether it is acceptable to use e-mail for personal use. Simple yet effective rules need to be introduced and guidelines need to be provided to staff regarding saving and deleting e-mails.

It is also important that the organization implementing a Corporate E-mail Policy embarks upon a strategy of organizationwide user education and training regarding the policy. It is simply not enough to place the "new" Corporate E-mail Policy on the organization's intranet with a link on the front page to the new e-mail policy. The introduction of any such policy needs to be backed up with full user support in the way of education and training programs.

E-mail Is Not an IT Issue; It's a Business Issue

It is important to remember that the management of e-mail is not an IT issue but a business issue. It is simply not enough for the organization's IT function to put the technology in place for managing e-mails and then have the organization accept (blindly) that e-mails are now managed. Instead, the management of e-mail is a business issue that, together with the Corporate E-mail Policy, represents a change in the way the organization works with and retains e-mail.

Laws, Regulatory Compliance, and E-mails

Because e-mails are business records, the same laws that apply to other records also apply to them. Laws such as Freedom of Information, Data Protection, and The Privacy Act all have an impact on business communications such as e-mail, fax, instant messaging services, and other written and electronic methods used to communicate both within and between organizations, and among organizations, their customers, and any other individuals.

The exact laws and regulations that apply to organizational e-mails will depend upon the country that the organization is based in, as well as the industry that the organization operates in. However, in the United States and United Kingdom, there are a core set of laws that organizations need to comply with regarding e-mails and related communications. In the United States, the Freedom of Information Act and The Privacy Act 1974 apply, whereas in the United Kingdom, the Freedom of Information

Act 2000 and Data Protection Act 1998 apply to both e-mails and related communications, and all other business records.

Classifying and Indexing E-mails

E-mails should be uploaded to the document repository as other documents and records are. Integration between e-mail client software and the EDRM system makes the uploading of e-mails easier for the users to do. E-mails should also be classified as public, team, or private. Those classified as public would be available for anyone in the organization to view, whereas e-mails classified as team would be available only to the users' team who classified the e-mail, and private e-mails would be classified as private, only available for viewing by the particular individual who has archived it.

Although e-mails can be classified as public, team, or private, system administrators and other authorized users should have the ability to search for and retrieve all e-mails regardless of whether they are classified as private or team. This will ensure that all e-mails can be retrieved and are accessible to the organization as a whole in case circumstances dictate that they need to be retrieved.

The E-mail Document Type

The E-mail Document Type will be used throughout the organization to store copies of e-mails in the EDRM document repository. The e-mail document type will need to include the following fields: From, To, Cc, Bcc, Sent/Received, Date, Subject, and Content. These are the fields found on e-mails that are received by the users in the organization, and hence will need to be replicated on the e-mail document type. Figure 8.1 illustrates the fields, field type, and size of the e-mail document type. The field sizes of the e-mail document type need to be of a suitable length to accommodate e-mails that are sent to multiple addresses, and the content field needs to be capable of storing text and other content commonly received in e-mails.

Searching and Retrieving E-mails

When searching for and retrieving e-mails, we need to decide whether the EDRM will offer separate searching facilities or include searches within the basic and advanced search facilities. It would most probably be best

Field Name	Data Type	Length	Format
From	Alphanumeric	255	
To	Alphanumeric	255	
Cc	Alphanumeric	255	
BCc	Alphanumeric	255	
Subject	Alphanumeric	255	
Content	Alphanumeric	Variable	
Date	Date Time		Depends on country's format
Sent/Received	Boolean		

Figure 8.1 E-mail document type.

for most organizations to include searches for e-mails within the basic and advanced searches as this would encourage a more transparent mechanism for searching across all business records, regardless of which document type they are. The basic searches discussed in Chapter 6 should include the ability to search across e-mails as well as other document types, whereas the advanced search, by its very definition, should provide a facility for searching just e-mail document types.

Retaining E-mails

There are many influencing factors that need to be considered before implementing a retention policy concerning e-mails, and organizations need to develop sensible retention and deletion policies that both comply with the laws and regulations that the organization needs to comply with as well as those that fit in with the organization's own specific needs and requirements.

One particular approach that can be taken to retain e-mails is to introduce an auto deletion facility of 30, 60, or 90 days if an e-mail is not archived before that time. However, this approach relies on the users to archive e-mails and, if users do not archive them, this approach to retaining e-mails would fail, as they would then be deleted.

Chapter 9

Records Management and Records Management Policies

Defining the records management policy for your organization is one the largest processes associated with the implementation of electronic document and records management systems (EDRMS) and covers topics such as retention schedules, archiving, security, auditing, and storage media, as well as creating and defining a records management statement for your organization.

There are also a plethora of standards associated with records management; some of these have been discussed in Chapter 3, Standards and Legislation; however, we will be further discussing records management standards in this chapter, as well.

What Constitutes a Record?

Chapter 2, Fundamentals of EDRMS, gave the definition of a record as per the *Oxford Dictionary of English*. However, we have to define what exactly is a record when related to EDRMS.

A record in an EDRM system is essentially a file that gives an evidential account of either a whole incident or part of an incident that occurred in the past. The record provides the factual information concerning that incident.

Because records contain factual information that occurred in the past, records must not be altered or changed in any way whatsoever.

A record can exist on any type of media. Most often records are scanned into the EDRM document repository as from historic paper records; however, records can also originate from letters, e-mails, faxes, word-processed document files, any and all computer files, and even Morse code transmissions.

When Do Documents Become Records?

Before we ask the question of when do documents become records, we have to first define what is a document as it relates to the EDRM system. A document can be considered to be any file, whether it is text-based, picture based, or any other type of format, which is under the control of an EDRM system. When a document is under the control of the EDRM system, the document can be changed and modified by authorized users, whereas a record cannot be changed or modified at all.

A document becomes a record when that particular document is archived. A document can be archived at any time but once a document is archived then no further changes can be made to the document. There are also a number of scenarios where a document becomes a record. For example, consider the scenario where a team is collectively working on a report. Once that report has been finalized and is ready to be submitted to the customer of the report, then a particular version number, e.g., 1.0, can be assigned to the report document, and it can be archived. If the team wishes to make any further changes to the report then a new copy of the report would be opened and assigned a new version number, e.g., 2.0. This would ensure that the original report, version 1.0, would remain intact as a historical record of the report as it existed at version 1.0 while still allowing the team to work on the report document, updating version 2.0.

Another scenario to consider in which documents become records is when a document goes through a workflow process and then becomes a record. For example, consider a loan application form that is received by a financial services company. Connected to the loan application form will be a workflow process to process the loan applications. In order for a loan application to be approved there will be a number of steps that the loan application will need to proceed through in the workflow. At any stage in the workflow the loan application could be refused. Once the loan application has been refused, and the loan application document is no longer in the workflow process — hence, the loan application document is subject no further changes — the refused loan application document can be archived as a record. If the loan application is successful, then again, once all the workflow process stages have been completed, the loan application document can be archived as record. Hence, to sum up, once a document has been through all the workflow process stages and is subject to no more workflow process stages or any other changes, only then can the document be archived as a record.

Retention Schedules

Retention schedules are concerned with the length of time an organization will retain records within the system's document repository. This depends on many factors, the most important being legislative issues, such as privacy laws and data protection laws, as well as freedom of information laws. Certain departments may decide that although there is no legislative reason why they should keep records for, let's say, no longer than seven years, they may, in fact, decide that they want to retain certain records indefinitely for their own record keeping and reference.

Archiving, security, and retention schedules are all tightly coupled and integrated together. An archived record is a record that has been filed within an EDRMS document repository, and therefore the record may be archived with certain security access levels, depending on the record's sensitivity. Once the record has been archived, that particular record is now retained by the EDRMS, hence the need for retention schedules. Once this time has expired from the date the record has been first archived, then it can be completely deleted from the system or moved to an off-line storage media.

Retention schedules will need to be devised for every single document type used within the EDRMS solution. Hence, two different records from the same department or team may be required to be retained for different periods of time. For example, legislation may require a Health and Safety Letter be retained for seven years, while legislation may require a Health and Safety Accident Form, such as the report of an injury or dangerous occurrence form, to be retained indefinitely.

The retention of records should happen automatically. Once records have been archived, scanned, categorized or indexed, the system should automatically retain the record based on the document type. Every document type needs to have its retention time period associated with it, e.g., seven years for a Health and Safety Letter, indefinitely for a Health and Safety Accident Form.

Once the retention time period for a record has expired, then it needs to be automatically removed from the system by either being completely destroyed or moved to off-line storage, depending upon the organization's records management policy statement.

Off-Line Storage Media

While records are being retained within the EDRMS document repository they reside on a server's hard disk, normally an array of hard disks; however, once the time approaches for records to be deleted, as specified by the retention schedules, then the organization has different options to consider. The records could be completely destroyed (being completely removed from the system) or the records could be moved to off-line storage. If records are moved to off-line storage, then they would be available for future reference, hence the records have still been retained.

Off-line storage media is available in many different formats such as CD-ROM, DVD-ROM, or tape; again, depending on the organization's specific needs as set out in the records management policy statement.

Archiving

The archiving of documents and records is tightly coupled to security and retention schedules. For example, when a particular record is archived within the EDRMS document repository the record has been archived as a result of the retention schedule specifying that the record's particular document type must be retained for a specific length of time; therefore retention schedules specify the length of time records should be retained.

With regards to the relationship between archiving and security, whenever a record is archived security settings will need to be applied to the record; i.e., the records may be restricted to certain individuals or departments within the organization, so that only these individuals, teams, or departments can view the records, or even see that the records exist in the first place.

Other records may be archived and have their security settings set to public view, so that they are accessible to anybody within the organization; on the other hand, sensitive information may only be accessible to certain individuals or departments in the organization.

The records management policy statement will also need to define when a document becomes a record. A document becomes a record when that particular document is archived and is no longer subject to any changes.

Security

In defining the records management statement, security needs to be an integral part of both the statement as well as being built into the EDRMS solution, and not merely added on as an afterthought. Security needs to be applied for specific groups of users and individual users at the document and records level of the system. Security access permissions also need to be defined so that individual users or groups of users have different access rights to the same records. At other times there may be a need to completely restrict access to a certain set of records all together, including the ability for unauthorized users in the organization to not even see that those documents or records exist, except for those users to whom access has been specifically granted, as such would be the case with highly classified documents and records within an organization.

Security access permissions normally allow an authorized system administrator to configure access to both individual files (documents or records) and also folders and sections within the EDRM document repository.

Auditing

As mentioned previously in Chapter 2, Fundamentals of EDRMS, auditing is an integral component of both EDM and ERM systems. An EDRMS solution must have the ability to provide an audit trail of who has accessed both documents and records in terms of the individual person who has initially categorized and indexed the record, and who has accessed the record and on what date, the time, and location.

As well as providing an accurate audit trail, an EDRMS solution also needs to keep previous versions of documents within the document repository so that other users such as administrators are able to access and view the changes that have been made to documents over the course of time.

Further Legislation and Standards on the Retention and Deletion of Documents

As mentioned previously in Chapter 1, whenever any organization stores information and data, certain legislative requirements must be met. Organizations are also required by law to retain records concerning other organizations or individuals for a certain period of time.

The actual amount of time that an organization is required to retain records depends on the type of records stored and the law of the particular country the organization is based in; however, certain legal records need to be kept on file indefinitely.

There is also the issue of whether both documents and records stored electronically can be used in a court of law if the paper version of the document or record does not exist. Legislation depends upon the country and organization in which the EDRMS has been implemented and, secondly, on the type of documents or records being stored.

Chapter 10

User Interfaces, Mobile Working and Remote Access

The design of the user interface of an EDRMS solution is one of the most important factors in the success of the system. A well-designed, easy-to-use, and intuitive user interface is needed in order for the staff within the organization to adopt the new system favorably. User interfaces generally come in two different styles for a Windows client and a Web client.

In this chapter we will be discussing both Windows clients and Web clients as well as the aspects that make up good user interface functionality. There will also be a review of the different types of remote access devices available for users of the EDRM system while away from the office.

This chapter also discusses the effect on the user interface when using remote access devices such as personal digital assistants (PDAs), which is why these two subjects are being discussed together.

The windows client user interface is made up of windows and forms that reside on the desktop of users' PCs, also referred to as a "thick client," while the Web client, also referred to as a "thin client," runs through a browser window, such as Microsoft Internet Explorer, Netscape Navigator, Opera, or Mozilla FireFox.

The vast majority of EDRMS software vendors include both Windows and Web clients with their product offerings. Both the Windows client and the Web client have advantages and disadvantages in their use.

Advantages of the Windows Client

The advantages of using the Windows client are that it offers the user the greatest level of functionality and flexibility. Functions such as sorting a list of documents and records into a predetermined order such as date order or alphabetical order can be done much quicker than when using a Web client running through a browser window. Accessing and viewing documents would be accomplished faster than using a Web client as Windows forms can generally transmit and handle data much faster than Web browsers. A Windows client would also offer the user greater detail with regards to the functionality that can be achieved as Windows forms offer greater functionality than Web-based applications.

Disadvantages of the Windows Client

The disadvantages of the Windows client are that they require software to be installed on each individual PC within the organization, i.e., the Windows client is the software that has to be installed on the PC. This is becoming less of an issue currently with the automated rollouts that occur in organizations; however, it still means that there is an additional piece of software on every single PC throughout the organization, which does run the risk, no matter how small, of failing and requiring maintenance to be carried out on that individual PC.

Another point to bear in mind is that a Windows client will often consume more resources in terms of memory, processor resources, and hard disk space than a Web client, which means that organizations have to evaluate the current specification of their standard desktop PCs in order to check if they meet the minimum specification required to adequately run the Windows client.

If the PC's specification does not meet the minimum specification then this would mean upgrading all PCs within the organization, which could be a very costly process. Upgrades to the Windows client would also involve upgrading the software on every single PC.

Advantages of the Web Client

The major advantages of the Web client are that you do not need to install separate software, as with the Windows client, on every single user PC in the organization; instead, all that is required is a program shortcut, placed on the desktop of every PC that will fire up a Web browser and launch the EDRMS Web client. This has the added benefit of not having to maintain extra software as the Web browser is delivering the Web client by accessing a Web application on a Web server. Hence, any changes made to the Web client application are made to the files on the Web server and not the individual client PCs. Thus, changes made on the Web server will be reflected immediately in the Web clients running on the PCs.

Disadvantages of the Web Client

The disadvantages of the Web client are that it does not offer the same degree of flexibility and functionality that a Windows client offers. For example, sorting a list of documents into date order or sorting them alphabetically would often involve the page being refreshed, which involves communication with the Web server, which in turn makes this process slower than if it had been carried out using a Windows client. Accessing and viewing documents and records would also be slower and more cumbersome as the Web browser would have to first render the page to be displayed, as well as load the document viewing application in order to view the images of the document.

Which User Interface? Windows Client or Web Client?

As discussed above, both the Windows clients and Web client have their respective advantages and disadvantages regarding their use and function-ality. The vast majority of EDRMS software vendors offer both WIndows and Web clients with their products so it generally depends on the organization as to which user interface they employ.

As no two organizations are the same, no matter how similar they may be with regards to their specific industry sector, the choice between employing a Windows client or Web client depends on many factors such as the level of computer literacy among the users in the organization and the resources of the IT support department, among many others.

Aspects of Good User Interface Design

There are several factors that go into providing an easy-to-use and intuitive user interface; these are listed in Figure 10.1 and are discussed below:

Displaying More than One Document or Record

The user interface should be able to display more than one document or record at once and should be able to effectively allow the user to view

- Displaying more than one document or record
- Displaying metadata associated with a document or record
- Navigating through the folder structure
- Search facilities
- Comparing different document or record versions
- Being able to access the document or records history as provided by an audit trail

Figure 10.1 Aspects of good user interface design.

as many documents or records as they need to view or as the resources, in terms of available memory, on their desktop PC allows.

The ability to view more than one document or record at once also allows the user to compare documents and records, cross referencing between them as well being able to quickly and easily view all documents or records connected with a particular case or incident. For example, if a user was viewing a record that is a planning application, it is more efficient to allow them to have other documents and records open on their desktop that are connected with the planning application, such as letters, building plans, surveyors reports, architect reports, etc. Opening one document or record, closing it, and then opening the next is a time-consuming process, which would also hinder the user's ability to cross-reference between the documents and records of that particular case.

Displaying Metadata Associated with a Document or Record

Having the option to be able to display the metadata associated with a document or record in the same window that displays the document or record is part of good user interface design, as it allows the user to see a snapshot of what the document or record is about very quickly without sifting through the whole document or record.

Navigating through the Folder Structure

Users should be able to browse and navigate through the folder structure easily in order to locate document and records or groups of documents or records. This offers users another facility, beside the search functions that allows them to find documents and records. Although users should be allowed to navigate the folder structure, only administrative users and other authorized users should be able to create new folders within the folder structure.

Search Facilities

Easy-to-use search facilities are an absolute must with any EDRMS implementation. Easy access to the search facilities is required as well as good presentation of the search facilities and good presentation of the search results listing, as discussed in Chapter 6, Search and Retrieval.

Accessing the Document or Records History

The ability for authorized users to access a document or records history is an important function that is connected to accountability for changes made to documents. Authorized users should be able to easily view a documents or records history by performing a simple function such as right-clicking on a document or record file, and then selecting view history from a list of menu options. The document or record history screen should then provide the user with a list of document versions, listing important information such as the date the document was created, the date the document was modified, and which user made the changes to the document. The user should also be able to select two different document versions and compare them side-by-side for comparison.

Comparing Different Document Versions

Being able to compare different document versions side by side is a useful feature that allows users to quickly and easily see the change that has occurred with documents. This is a useful feature to have which ties in with being able to a view a documents history through the audit trail, because as soon the list of document versions has been produced the user can select two different document versions and then view the changes that have been made to them side by side.

Mobile Working

There will be times when a user needs access to the documents and records held within the EDRMS document repository but is away from the office. By setting up remote access to the system via devices such as laptop computers and PDAs with data connections, we can give staff who are off-site access to the EDRMS.

In the case of laptop computers, the user interface can remain the same as a desktop PC; however when using PDAs, the user interface that is delivered to the PDA will have to be quite significantly different from the user interface used on either a desktop or laptop PC.

User Interfaces and PDAs

A user interface designed for a PDA will be significantly different from the user interface displayed on a desktop or laptop PC. This is because of the limitations of the PDA device in terms of screen size and the software that is able to run on the PDA devices.

The PDA user interface will be a cut down version of the Web-client user interface that runs on desktop PCs. A significant amount of the functionality associated with the Web-client user interface will be missing when accessing the EDRM system using a PDA device.

It will still be possible to view documents and records on a PDA device; however, these images will need to be reduced in size in order to fit on the PDA screen, while allowing the user to zoom in to specific areas of the image. The user interface running on a PDA would also take a different approach regarding displaying documents or records and render them in a format suitable for display on a PDA, such as is accomplished with e-books.

Off-Line Working

There will be occasions when users are out of the office and will need to work with a set of documents or records connected to a particular incident or case, but may not be able to use a data connection where they are located. In cases like this we need to employ off-line working methods that allow the user to work with those documents or records off-line, i.e., without being connected to the EDRMS.

Off-line working can be achieved by allowing the users to download copies of the documents or records to a laptop PC. This would also check-out those documents that they have downloaded on the laptop to prevent other users from making changes to the documents during the time they are working with the documents, thus avoiding synchronization issues when the users return to the office.

This would then enable the user to effectively work with those documents without being connected to the organization's network or having access to the EDRMS. Although the users are off-site, if they need to make changes to the documents they can make changes to the local copy of the documents on their laptop PC and upon their return to the office would be able to synchronize the documents they have on their laptop

PC with the documents held in the EDRMS document repository, effectively updating the documents in the document repository if they have been amended while the user has been away from the office.

Chapter 11

Scanning Historical Documents and Records

During the implementation of the EDRMS solution, a project plan will need to be put in place in order to scan, classify, and index the organization's current paper files and folders. Most medium and large organizations have lots of historical paper files and documents in at least one filing room if not many more; hence, a separate project is needed to archive both historical documents and records.

Deciding what to scan and what not to scan is a complicated process that needs to take account of many factors such as retention schedules, cost, time, planning, and other factors. Initially, the organization may want to scan all historic documents; however, in practice, scanning all historic documents could well be a very costly and time-consuming process that may be impractical to undertake.

Processes

There are three main processes involved with setting up a scanning project. These are preparation, scanning, classifying, indexing, and quality assurance. Preparation for scanning involves deciding which documents to scan and which documents to discard. Scanning, classification, and indexing is the process of getting the documents uploaded into the EDRMS document repository, and quality assurance involves the systematic checking of uploaded documents and records to make sure they have been accurately scanned in terms of image quality, as well as classified and indexed correctly.

Preparation

The preparation process is primarily concerned with defining which historical records will be scanned and retained compared to those historic records that do not have any value to the organization anymore or are no longer required to be retained by law and therefore can be discarded.

Both the retention schedules previously defined for documents and records, and user consultation, should drive the preparation process. It is particularly important to consult users before embarking on the scanning of historic documents and records as not doing so could mean that documents or records that are currently being used by staff, which may be relied upon for the day-to-day tasks, are not scanned into the system if they do not fall within the retention schedules defined for those document types. For example, if the retention schedules specify that Health and Safety Letters only need to be retained for seven years, then if a particular user wants to keep certain Health and Safety Letters for longer, the act of effectively destroying those letters by not scanning them into the system may well encumber the user in performing certain tasks of their day-to-day job that may be associated and connected to the letters not scanned on to the system.

During the preparation process users should be consulted to ascertain which documents they require and which they do not require. The preparation process will also involve the systematic culling (discarding) of a department's paper documents and records. Once the paper documents and records have been suitably culled, the project can then move on to the scanning, classification, and indexing process; hence, the preparation process feeds this process.

Scanning, Classification, and Indexing

There are three separate tasks that are involved with uploading a document or record into the EDRMS solution. The scanning part of this process involves actually scanning the paper document or record so that it is rendered as an image file. Classification refers to classifying the scanned document or record, which is now an image file, as a particular document type, whereas indexing refers to inputting the correct metadata, such as dates, authors, subjects, etc., that are required to be associated with that document or record.

With regard to scanning, classifying, and indexing paper documents and records, there are different methods that may be used to accomplish this task. The scanning, classifying, and indexing of documents and records could be performed within the organization using existing staff in-house or the process could be outsourced to an external company to complete either on-site within the organization or off-site at the external companies' premises.

As well as completing the scanning, classification, and indexing tasks either entirely in-house or off-site, a hybrid approach can be taken. Thus, paper documents and records could be scanned and classified as certain document types off-site and indexed on-site. Outsourcing scanning and classification would, in most cases, allow the organization to complete the scanning and classification of paper documents and records in a very short time, as the organization could use the services of a specialist scanning bureau which would be using high capacity scanners in order to scan folders and their contents. Hence, if the organization implementing the EDRMS solution does not have high capacity scanning equipment, then this approach could save on time as well as cost. Indexing documents and records in-house would allow the organization to retain control over how documents and records are indexed and would make the quality assurance process much simpler as indexers and the staff carrying out the quality assurance process are in the same location.

On-Site Scanning, Classification, and Indexing

Undertaking the scanning, classification, and indexing of document and records on site at the organization's premises has the advantages of keeping all files and folders on-site within the organization, which enables files and folders to be retrieved by users if necessary. The on-site operation also gives the organization more control over the processes than if the task was be completed externally.

There are three approaches an organization can take with regards to resourcing the scanning, classification, and indexing process on site. The first is to use in-house staff in order to complete all scanning, classification, and indexing of documents. This approach has the benefits of not having to recruit temporary staff and also keeps costs down as remuneration does not need to be paid to outside staff. The disadvantages to this approach are, firstly, finding the right staff to scan, categorize, and index documents for any length of time, as the process is by nature quite tedious and laborious. Secondly, it may be harder to enforce strict time scales and deadlines when working with in-house staff who may, in the first place, resent having to scan, classify, and index documents and records.

One option is to use external staff that have been recruited for the task of scanning, classifying, and indexing. With this approach you are more likely to recruit the type of personnel who are more suited to the task of scanning, classifying, and indexing documents and records as they have applied for the role in the first place; hence, it would also be easier to enforce stricter time scales and deadlines in order to get the task completed. The disadvantage with this approach is that these personnel would need to be hired and may involve higher costs to the organization as opposed to using existing personnel.

A second option is to employ a specialist company, a scanning bureau that will scan and index the organization's documents and records on site at the organization. This, then, shifts responsibility onto the scanning bureau in order to complete the task by a given time for fixed price. This is normally the most expensive of all the three options for on-site scanning and indexing; however, it removes the burden of scanning and indexing documents from within the organization.

The exact approach to take again depends upon the organization. Certain organizations may well have the resources in-house to complete the processes in an efficient manner, whereas other organizations will have to recruit externally for adept personnel in order to complete the scanning and indexing process. Another important factor to bear in mind is scanning and indexing capacity, as well as floor space. The organization will need to have adequate scanners as well as PCs connected to the scanners to accommodate the large volume of paper to be scanned and the floor space to house the scanners, PCs, and large volume of paper waiting to be scanned.

Off-Site Scanning, Categorization, and Indexing

Employing this option will result in the organization's paper files and folders being scanned off-site by an external company. The major disadvantage in this case is that should an individual within the organization require access to their files or folders currently in the process of being scanned and indexed, then it could take days in order to get the files back to the organization.

Off-site scanning and indexing does allow organizations to take advantage of offshore operations that may be able to scan and index at a much reduced cost compared to scanning and indexing within the country of origin. However, there are also risks associated with the management of outsourced operations, as well as data protection and privacy issues regarding the organization's information.

Taking into account the risks associated with off-site and offshore scanning and indexing, it would be a better option for most organizations to keep their files and folders in-house and choose one of the approaches listed for in-house scanning, categorization, and indexing of historical paper files and folders.

Training Needs of Scanning and Indexing Personnel

Another important factor to consider before the scanning, classification, and indexing process commences is that the personnel who are undertaking the task will need to be trained firstly in the use of the scanning and indexing software as well as trained in how to index certain document types.

In training users to index individual kinds of documents, the personnel responsible for categorizing and indexing these need to liaise with the key users in the departments where the documents originate. Initially, the key users should spend some length of time with the indexing personnel to ensure that the document types are properly and correctly indexed.

Quality Assurance

The quality assurance process is the last process associated with back scanning historical paper files and folders. As the name suggests, this process is concerned with systematically checking that paper documents and records have been satisfactorily scanned, classified as the correct document type, and then properly indexed with the correct metadata.

It would be too time consuming to check every single paper document and record that has been scanned and indexed for accuracy, so we need a method to ensure that documents and records are generally being scanned, classified, and indexed in the correct and proper manner. When the scanning, classifying, and indexing process has just started for a particular document type, such as Health and Safety, it is advantageous to check each scanned document and record for the first few days of scanning and indexing process, essentially while the scanning and index-ing personnel are getting used to indexing the "new" document types. Once those few days have passed and if the quality assurance operative is satisfied that the documents and records are being scanned, classified, and indexed in the proper and correct manner then the quality assurance process of checking could change focus and check ten random documents and the record of every hundred documents and records that have been scanned in. If, after quality checking the batch of documents and records, all ten documents and records have been satisfactorily scanned and indexed, then the batch of 100 documents and records would be deemed as having passed the quality assurance process. If on the other hand there are any errors at all in the random sample of ten documents that have been used for the quality assurance process, it is advisable to check through the complete batch for errors and then request that the scanning and indexing personnel rescan and index all those documents and records with errors on them.

Quality assurance is quite a time-consuming process and will need to have adequate human resources assigned. Quality assurance personnel will also need to work closely with the scanning and indexing personnel in order to effectively liaise and communicate regarding the process.

Running the Processes in Parallel

Organizing the three processes of preparation, scanning, classification, and indexing, as well as and quality assurance, so that they run in parallel is key to completing the scanning project in a timely manner. It is advantageous to organize the three processes so that preparation feeds the scanning, classification, and indexing process, which in turn feeds the quality assurance process, as shown in Figure 11.1 , with scanned images that do not pass the quality assurance process going back into the scanning, classification, and indexing process.

Case Study — Warrington NHS (National Health Service) Primary Care Trust (United Kingdom)

Warrington NHS Primary Care Trust consisted of 13 departments that were relocating to a single building. However, no record storage space had been allocated, which meant that 25,000 patient medical records had to be stored somewhere.

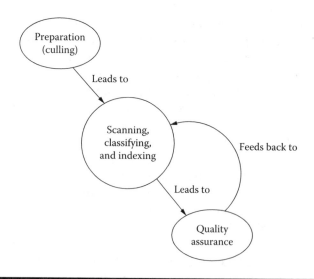

Figure 11.1   Scanning historical documents and records process.

Requirements

In October 2004 Ellison began consultation with Warrington NHS Primary Care Trust and came up with a digital capture solution that enabled the NHS trust to convert all its paper patient records into an electronic format available across the allied health professional services (AHP) by March 2005. The solution also had to be scalable to cope with the growing demands of further medical records and also fit into the wider requirements of the NHS Primary Care Trust under the CfH (Connecting for Health) program, where the Computer Services Corporation (CSC) had been appointed as the local service provider to the Northwest of England.

The proposed solution also had to be capable of including additional departments, capturing correspondence, and managing complaints. The solution also had to be compliant with both the Freedom of Information Act and Data Protection Act, and of key importance was that the solution, would involve the minimum of disruption for users of the records which were being scanned into the new system.

Solution

The first phase of the implementation involved the installation of the community patient administration system (PAS). At the same time Ellison began the off-site patient record conversion, which consisted of an eight-stage fully auditable and secure process.

Ellison collected the records from all 13 departments' records stores during an eight-day period. The records were securely transported to a secure scanning facility, where each medical record was bar-coded and entered into a bespoke tracking system to ensure that records could be located while they were in the process of being scanned. Records were scanned in compliance with BIP 0008, the Code of Practice for Legal Admissibility, and evidential weight of information stored electronically. The records were indexed using the records' NHS patient number, allowing them to be easily transferred and integrated into the NHS Trusts system, once the department had relocated to the new building. After this the original paper records were archived.

The conversion of paper patient records to electronic patient records has enabled the Warrington Primary Care Trust to save costs associated with the storage of paper records, as well as increasing efficiency within the organization.

Part 3

A FRAMEWORK FOR EDRMS

Chapter 12

Project Management

With the initial thoughts of starting up a project to implement an EDRMS solution it is important to consider working with a defined project methodology or framework. This chapter will take a look at two popular project management methods: PRINCE2™ and PMBOK.

PRINCE2™ (**PR**ojects **IN** **C**ontrolled **E**nvironments) is a project management methodology developed in the United Kingdom, whereas PMBOK (**P**roject **M**anagement **BO**dy of **K**nowledge) is a collection of processes and knowledge that provides guidance on best practice within project management.

Although this book is not primarily concerned with project management, it is concerned with effectively implementing EDRMS; hence, effective project management, along with all the key documents as well adequate Change Management practices are essential ingredients in the implementation of any computer system, whether it be EDRMS or not. Therefore, the rest of this book is devoted to these topics, as they are essential to the successful implementation of EDRMS.

PRINCE2™

PRINCE2™ is a trademark of the U.K. Office of Government Commerce.

It is a project management methodology that is concerned with the control of projects within organizations. The Central Computer and Telecommunications Agency (CCTA), which is now part of the Office of Government Commerce (OGC), originally developed PRINCE in 1989 as a U.K. government standard for IT project management.

PRINCE is widely used in the public and private sectors in the United Kingdom and has become a project management standard. It was originally developed for IT projects but the PRINCE methodology has been used with other non-IT projects as well.

The latest version is PRINCE2™, which is a process-based approach to project management that provides a scalable method for managing all types of projects.

Each process in the PRINCE2 methodology is defined with clear inputs and outputs as well as objectives and activities to be achieved. The methodology describes how a project should be divided into stages with control of resources as well as regular process monitoring during each of the project's stages. Projects run according to the PRINCE2 methodology are product-based, which means that project plans are focused on delivering results.

PRINCE2 projects are driven by the project's business case. The business case justifies the organization's need for the existence of the project. The business case is reviewed at regular intervals throughout the project's life to ensure that business objectives are being met.

The following section describes both the PRINCE processes and components in detail. Further information on PRINCE2 can be found online at http://www.ogc.gov.uk/prince2.

PRINCE2 Processes

PRINCE2 contains eight separate processes that will be discussed in greater detail below. Any project that uses the PRINCE2 methodology will need to address each process in some form, however the extent to which a particular process is utilized depends upon the individual project; however, the PRINCE2 methodology encourages the project manager to tailor each process to their project's own specific needs.

Each process has its own aims and objectives, and produces a series of products such as the risk log, issues log, and lessons-learned log. The products are essentially documents that record specific topic areas within the project such as "risks and issues." A further discussion on the products produced by processes will be provided after the discussion around processes and components.

Each of the processes described below also contain other processes, and hence each main process is made up of other smaller processes within the main process. Each main process is assigned initials such as SU for "starting up a project," whereas the subprocesses contained within the SU process then have the initials of SU assigned to them as well as a number suffixing the initials, such as SU1, SU2, SU3, as well their individual process name. All eight main processes follow this naming convention for both the name of their own processes and the processes they contain.

It is important to note that the PRINCE2 processes are not sequential processes, whereby a process starts and then ends before another process starts. Instead, many of the processes run in parallel, with some processes running over the entire project life cycle and others only running for a specific time within the project life cycle.

Starting up a Project (SU)

The SU process is considered to be a preproject process that exists purely in order to ensure that the prerequisites for initiating the project are in place. This process requires that a Project Mandate be in place. The Project Mandate should consist of the reason for the project as well as the result of product. For example, in the case of EDRMS, the reasons for starting up the project would be to increase productivity and save costs, while complying with records-keeping legislation. The result of the project would be a fully functional and implemented EDRMS solution that complies with record-keeping legislation that has increased productivity and saved costs within the organization.

The SU process is also concerned with appointing the project management team, the project brief, the approach of the project specifically with regards to how the solution will be provided, the project customer(s) expectations in terms of quality, any risks associated with the project in terms of a risk log, as well as initiating the project using a Stage Plan. This process contains six other processes that are shown in Figure 12.1.

Process Code	Process Name
SU1	Appointing a Project Board Executive and a Project Manager
SU2	Designing a Project Management Team
SU3	Appointing a Project Management Team
SU4	Preparing a Project Brief
SU5	Defining a Project Approach
SU6	Planning an Initiation Stage

Figure 12.1   Starting up a project (SU).

Directing a Project (DP)

The DP process runs from the end of the SU process and in parallel with all other processes until the project comes to a close. The purpose of this process is to keep the project board informed regarding the progress of the project. The project board are a group of senior people within the organization who have responsibility for the project and who will ultimately make all the important decisions regarding the project. This process contains five other processes that occur at various stages of the project lifecycle. These five processes are shown in Figure 12.2.

Initiating a Project (IP)

The IP process is concerned with the in-depth details of the project. This process is primarily concerned with producing the Project Initiation Document (PID) that defines the intricate details of the project, commonly referred to as the who, why, what, where, and how of the project.

The PID should include the plan and cost of the project as well as providing justification that a viable Business Case exists for the project. The PID should also define how the required quality of the product produced by the project will be achieved as well as ensuring that the investment of resources for the project is justified and not outweighed by the risks of the project.

The process should also encourage the Project Board to take ownership of the project and agree to the commitment of resources required for the project and any subsequent stages of the project. This process will also create three other blank products: the Quality Log, the Issues Log, and the Lessons Learned Log, which will be used throughout the project lifecycle. The IP process contains six other processes that are shown in Figure 12.3.

Process Code	Process Name
DP1	Authorizing Initiation
DP2	Authorizing a Project
DP3	Authorizing a Stage or Exception Plan
DP4	Giving Ad Hoc Direction
DP5	Confirming Project Closure

Figure 12.2 Directing a project (DP).

Process Code	Process Name
IP1	Planning Quality
IP2	Planning a Project
IP3	Refining the Business Case and Risks
IP4	Setting up Project Controls
IP5	Setting up Project Files
IP6	Assembling a Project Initiation Document

Figure 12.3   Initiating a project (IP).

Managing Stage Boundaries (SB)

The primary purpose of the SB process is to produce the information necessary for the Project Board to decide whether the project should continue or be terminated.

The aims and objectives of this process are to inform and assure the project board that all the products and deliverables of the current Stage Plan have been completed as specified and provide the information that the project board needs to assess the continued viability of the project, as well as providing the project board with the information needed to approve the completion of the current stage of the project and authorize the next stage of the project. This process also records and monitors any lessons learned from the current stage of the project in order to help further stages in the project.

The products and deliverables of this process is the End Stage Report, which contains information of the achievements on the current stage of the project and the current Stage Plan performance against the original Stage Plan performance, allowing the project board to evaluate the progress of the project. Approval will also be sought for the next Stage Plan of the project, and a revised Project Plan will be developed and delivered to the project board, as well as changes, if any, to the project management team in terms of the structure or staffing of the team. The updated Risk Log, together with the revised Business Case and the Lessons Learned Log is also used by the Project Board to assess and review the ongoing viability of the project. The SB process consists of six other processes, shown in Figure 12.4.

Process Code	Process Name
SB1	Planning a Stage
SB2	Updating a Project Plan
SB3	Updating a Project Business Case
SB4	Updating the Risk Log
SB5	Reporting Stage End
SB6	Producing an Exception Plan

Figure 12.4   Managing stage boundaries (SB).

Controlling a Stage (CS)

This process is primarily concerned with managing and controlling the day-to-day tasks and events that occur with the project. Throughout this process the project manager will be involved in multiple cycles of authorizing work to be undertaken and getting progress reports (both formally and informally) on how specific tasks are progressing. The project manager will need to constantly review the current situation, and be aware of any changes that are occurring and are deviating the project away from its current plan.

This process also covers the risk and issue management of the project and the project's daily work. Hence, this process results in a number of products, multiple times, throughout the project. These products include Work Packages, Highlight Reports, Project Issues, an updated Risk Log, and regularly updated Stage Plan. The Controlling a Stage process consists of nine other processes that are shown in Figure 12.5.

Managing Product Delivery (MP)

The primary objective of this process is to ensure that the planned products of the project are created and delivered by the project team. The process aims to ensure that the Team Manager communicates details of the project's work packages to the project manager, as well as ensuring that the work on the products allocated to the project team has been duly authorized and agreed.

This process also ensures that the work undertaken on the project conforms to the requirements and specifications detailed in the work packages as well as making sure the work meets the quality assurance

Process Code	Process Name
CS1	Authorizing Work Package
CS2	Assessing Progress
CS3	Capturing Project Issues
CS4	Examining Project Issues
CS5	Reviewing Stage Status
CS6	Reporting Highlights
CS7	Taking Corrective Action
CS8	Escalating Project Issues
CS9	Receiving Work Package

Figure 12.5 Controlling a stage (CS).

Process Code	Process Name
MP1	Accepting a Work Package
MP2	Executing a Work Package
MP3	Delivering a Work Package

Figure 12.6 Managing product delivery (MP).

criteria specified. The process also needs to ensure that work progresses to schedule and approval is obtained for the completed products of the project. This process includes works in conjunction with the CS process and consists of three other processes as shown in Figure 12.6.

The products created and updated by this process are Team Plans and Quality Log updates, which give the project manager an overview of the quality assessment work being carried out. Any project issues identified also need to be recorded in the Issues Log and Risk Log. The MPD process also creates Checkpoint reports, which are regular progress reports from the Team Manager given to the Project Manager.

Closing a Project (CP)

The aim of this process is provide a controlled close to the project, either at the end of the project or earlier, in the case of the project being closed

Process Code	Process Name
CP1	Decommissioning a Project
CP2	Identifying Follow-on Actions
CP3	Evaluating a Project

Figure 12.7 Closing a project (CP).

prematurely. The process involves the project manager making sure that all the steps are in place and in order, and reporting this to the project board so that they may give their approval for the project to close.

In order for project managers to confirm to the project board that the project is ready to close, they will have to check the project's results against the aims and objectives set out in the PID, as well as obtaining sign-off from the project's customer. The project manager will also have to report to the project board the extent to which the project's products have been handed over and accepted by the customer, as well as confirming that any maintenance or other operational arrangements have been put in place to support the product(s) delivered by the project, and ensuring that sufficient training has been provided. This process contains three other processes as shown in Figure 12.7.

In order to properly close the project this process requires that an End Project Report is produced, along with any recommendations for future work, contained in a Follow-on Actions Recommendations document. The project manager will also need to capture lessons learned from the project and complete the Lessons Learned Report as well as archiving project files, producing a Post-Project Review Plan, and finally notifying the host organization on the intention to disband the project team and release the resources previously used by the project team.

Planning

The planning process is a process that occurs over and over again and runs in parallel with other processes, playing an important role in the planning of processes such as Planning an Initial Stage, which is part of the SP Process, and Planning a Project, which is part of the IP process. The planning process also plays an important role in the Planning a Stage, Updating a Project Plan, and Producing an Exception Plan processes, which are all contained within the SB process. The Planning process also plays a role in the Accepting a Work Package process that is part of the Managing Product Delivery process.

Process Code	Process Name
PL1	Designing a Plan
PL2	Defining and Analyzing Products
PL3	Identifying Activities and Dependencies
PL4	Estimating
PL5	Scheduling
PL6	Analyzing Risks
PL7	Completing a Plan

Figure 12.8   Planning (CS).

The planning process produces the Product Checklist, which is a plan of the project's deliverables in terms of the products the project is scheduled to produce. The Product Checklist includes planned and actual dates for draft and quality-checked and approved products to be delivered by the project. The process also requires that the Risk Log be updated with any risk issues identified by this process. The Planning process includes seven other processes as shown in Figure 12.8.

The Components

The PRINCE2 methodology contains eight components: Business Case, Organization, Plans, Controls, Management of Risk, Quality in a Project Environment, Configuration Management, and Change Control.

The PRINCE2 processes and subprocesses contained within the processes use these components at various stages within the process. For example, the Business Case is a component that will be used by almost every single process in PRINCE2, as the Business Case is the document that drives the project, and is constantly referred to at regular stages in the project in order to confirm that the project is still justifiable. The Project Plan, part of the Plans component, is another document that will be referred to by almost every single process in PRINCE2™. All eight components are described below:

Business Case

The Business Case is the most important document in any PRINCE2 project as it is the Business Case that drives the project. The Business Case is produced at the start of the project, and if the Business Case cannot justify the project, then the project should cease and not go any further. If a justifiable Business Case exists at the beginning of the project, then the project should proceed. However, if the Business Case at any time during the project cannot justify the project's ongoing existence then the project should be terminated. Hence, the Business Case has failed to justify the project.

The Business Case details the reasons for the project based on cost saving to the organization and the expected business benefits versus cost of the project and business risks. The Business Case should detail the way in which the project will facilitate change throughout the organization. Chapter 13, The Business Case, contains a discussion of each of the components of a business case in greater detail.

Organization

The PRINCE2™ Project Management structure is based on the customer/supplier relationship model, with the supplier being the project board, project manager, team manager, and project team members that make up the project. The customer/supplier relationship model assumes that a project is being undertaken for a customer. This customer may be an internal customer based within the same organization as the project that is being undertaken, or the customer could be an external third party to the organization. The organization component aims to establish an effective project management structure in order to ensure the structured and systematic delivery of the project's products.

Plans

Plans in the PRINCE2 methodology are used for planning the activities that need to take place within each stage of the project in order to produce the required outputs from each stage. PRINCE2 plans need to include information such as the products that will be produced and the activities that are needed to produce those products, as well as the activities needed to validate the quality of products. Plans will also need to specify the resources, people, and time needed in order to achieve the desired outcome, i.e., the product, as well as determining the interrelated dependencies between activities. Plans also need to specify when activities will happen and detail checkpoints in the progress of activities for monitoring, as well as agreeing tolerances, in terms of time and resources needed for the completion of the activities of the plan.

PRINCE2 uses three levels of plans, all which need approval from the project board. The three levels of plan are the Project Plan, Stage Plan, and Team Plan. In cases where a Stage Plan or Team Plan exceeds predetermined tolerances (time or money), then an Exception Plan can be produced to replace the plan that has exceeded its tolerances.

The Project Plan forms part of the Project Initiation Document (PID) and is the only mandatory plan in PRINCE2, providing the Business Case with project costs and used by the Project Board in order to monitor the actual costs and project progress.

The Stage Plan is normally produced for each stage that has been identified by the Project Plan, although producing a Stage Plan is not a mandatory requirement of PRINCE2. Each Stage Plan, is normally produced as the end of the current stage draws close. Stage Plans are normally used by Project Managers to monitor day-to-day progress of a stage.

Team Plans are normally created for large and more complex projects and are generally created at the same time as Stage Plans. In cases where different teams are responsible for completing different activities, Team Plans break down the activities of a specific stage into chunks of work to be completed by the teams.

Controls

Controls are used in a PRINCE2 project to ensure that the project remains on schedule within the agreed timescales and budget, and is producing the required products, hence keeping in line with the project's Business Case. Therefore, controls are associated with every aspect of a PRINCE2 project, from Project Start-Up through Controlled Close.

Many of the controls in PRINCE2 are event driven, with the control occurring when a specific event in the project has occurred, such as the end of a stage. There are a number of controls that PRINCE2 puts in place for the Project Board. These are Project Initiation, End Stage Assessments, Highlight Reports, Exception Reports, Exception Assessments, and Project Closure.

Project Initiation is concerned with whether the project should be undertaken. End Stage assessments allow the Project Board to assess the completion of a stage in terms of its success and also determine whether the project remains on course, while checking that the Business Case is still viable. Ultimately, the End Stage assessment determines if the project should proceed and move on to the next stage. Highlight Reports are regular progress reports produced for the Project Board during a stage, while Exception Reports provide an early warning to the Project Board of a stage running foul of agreed tolerances. Exception Assessments provides the Project Board with an opportunity to meet and review Exception Plans. Finally, Project Closure allows the Project to come to an orderly close, while reviewing whether the project has delivered everything expected and what lessons have been learned from the project.

Management of Risk

The Management of Risk also commonly referred to as Risk Management plays an important role in any project. There will be always be an element of risk when undertaking a project as the outcome of the project, no matter how well the project has been planned, is subject to many different variables. Hence, there is always a degree of uncertainty, i.e., risk, associated with the undertaking of a project.

PRINCE2 uses an approach to Risk Management in order to control the level of risk associated with a project, which starts off with Identifying the Risks associated with a project and then moves on to Evaluating the Risks and identifying suitable responses to the risks. The Risk Management process then selects, plans, and resources for risks and finally monitors and reports on risks, which are recorded in the project's Risk Log.

PRINCE2 employs Risk Ownership, which identifies an owner for each risk. The owner of a particular risk would normally be the person who is most able to monitor the risk and keep an eye on the risk. Commonly, Project Board members are appointed as "owners" of risks.

Quality in a Project Environment

PRINCE2 projects need to make sure that the products they are producing are fit for purpose, therefore assuring the products are produced to a certain quality. The approach that PRINCE2 takes to ensure this is termed Quality in a Project Environment, which in turn uses a Quality Management approach to manage the quality of products produced. Quality Management in PRINCE2 contains the following elements: Quality System, Quality Assurance, Quality Planning, and Quality Control.

The Quality System is the collection of procedures and processes that occur within the organization in order to implement Quality Management. If the customer is using a certain type of Quality System and the supplier another, then the project will either have to use one of these Quality Systems or a mixture of both. The customer and supplier simply cannot use different Quality Systems on the same project.

Quality Assurance is the method used to ensure that the end product produced by the project meets both quality and customer expectations and requirements. In order to assure that the Quality Assurance function remains objective, the Quality Assurance function should be both separate and independent from the project and the organization that is responsible for the project. If a separate and independent Quality Assurance body does not exist then the Project Assurance function can be incorporated into the quality assurance role in the project.

Quality Planning establishes the methods to be used for establishing and checking for quality. The PID defines the quality methods that are to be used for the project in the Project Quality Plan. The customer's expectation regarding quality needs to be understood and fully documented in the SU process. Additionally, each Stage Plan needs to specify the methods used for quality checking with the deliverance of each product.

Quality Control is the method used to ensure that products are examined to check if they meet the quality criteria specified.

Configuration Management

Configuration Management is the method used by PRINCE2 to control and manage the products produced by a project. The method Configuration Management uses in controlling and managing products is version control. By using a "baseline," products are essentially frozen at a particular period in time, normally after a certain stage or series of stages of the product's development has been completed. When a product is "baselined" it is assigned a version number. The "baselined" product with its version number allows products to be referenced as various stages of their development. For example, in the case of software development, an application would be "baselined," at various stages and have consecutive version numbers assigned to it. The project manager is then able to review or go back to the product, in this case the application, at any point in the application (product) development life cycle, by referring to the version numbers.

Configuration Management in PRINCE2™ consists of five basic elements. These are Planning, Identification, Control, Status Accounting, and Verification.

Planning is concerned with deciding the level at which Configuration Management is required and how it will be implemented. The Configuration Management Plan forms part of the Project Quality Plan and defines how the products will be stored, the filing and retrieval security needed for previous versions of products, how different versions of products will be identified, and who is in charge and responsible for the Configuration Management of the project's products.

Identification is concerned with providing unique identification to each product, and requires that each product needs to be identified by their project, the type of product, i.e., software, hardware, the product's name, and version number.

Control is concerned with keeping track of products, the products' status, protecting completed products or controlling any changes that are made to a completed product.

Status Accounting is concerned with keeping a written record of both current and historical data concerning each individual product produced by the project.

Verification is essentially an auditing exercise that is concerned with either proving or disproving that products' statuses are as they have been recorded in Configuration Management records.

Change Control

Change Control is the method used by PRINCE2 in order to manage change and change requests within projects. Once a project is under way, change requests are almost inevitable, hence each request for change has to be managed and handled in a controlled manner. If change or change requests are not controlled or managed, this can lead to potential issues with the project going off-track and deviating from the original specification. PRINCE2 records Change Requests as Project Issues.

The Change Control component in PRINCE2 records all requests for change as Project Issues. Project Issues need to be considered on the benefits they have for the entire project while also being evaluated against the Business Case. The risk of implementing a change request should be logged in the risk log and the risk, cost and time of implementing a change request needs to be considered, compared to the advantages and saving made.

PMBOK (Project Management Body of Knowledge)

PMBOK is a term used by the Project Management Institute to describe the sum of knowledge within the profession of project management. Hence, the PMBOK is a document produced by the Project Management Institute that includes a methodology that can be used for the vast majority of projects.

Project Management Knowledge Areas

There are nine knowledge areas within PMBOK that relate to specific areas of a specific project or project phase. These nine knowledge areas are listed below:

- Project Integration Management
- Project Scope Management

- Project Time Management
- Project Cost Management
- Project Quality Management
- Project Human Resource Management
- Project Communications Management
- Project Risk Management
- Project Procurement Management

These nine knowledge areas do not run sequentially one after the other, but instead run in parallel throughout the duration of the overall project. For example, Project Time Management is a knowledge area that will run throughout the course of the project, as project managers constantly review activities and their impact on various timescales of the project.

It is also important to realize that not all projects will use all these nine knowledge areas within their specific project, whereas other projects may use some knowledge areas more heavily than others. For example, with the development of an in-house EDRMS solution the project may not include the Project Procurement knowledge area, as the product is being developed in-house and does not need to be procured from an external supplier. Also, in the case of very small projects, which are entirely outsourced to external contractors where the project manager simply oversees and liaises with contractors, there will not be any need for the Project Human Resource Management knowledge area to be used. Thus, each individual project will use the knowledge areas in unique ways that aid that particular project, with knowledge areas running in parallel to suit the individual project.

The PMBOK defines five process groups each. Within the process groups there are individual processes that interact with each other across the nine knowledge areas. These five processes are listed below:

- Initiating Processes
- Planning Processes
- Executing Processes
- Controlling Processes
- Closing Processes

The processes of Planning, Executing, and Controlling often occur multiple times within a specific knowledge area and can also run in parallel until the desired outcome is achieved, upon which the closing process then closes down the specific knowledge area task.

Each of the processes interacts with each other using Inputs, Tools and Techniques, and Outputs. Inputs are documents or other events that make particular processes happen. Tools and Techniques are the activities that are applied to the inputs and are utilized in order to create the Output(s) required.

Project Phases

PMBOK recognizes that each project may contain one or more project phases. A project phase is a discrete section of an overall project, such as the design phase. The overall project is referred to as the project lifecycle.

The Five Process Groups

PMBOK groups all the processes contained within the knowledge areas into one of five groups. These groups are Initiating Processes, Planning Processes, Executing Processes, Controlling Processes, and Closing Processes.

The Initiating processes are the processes used to start a particular project or phase of a project. This is the process that recognizes that there is a need for the project.

The Planning processes are used for planning different sections of the project such as costs, human resources, and timescales, among other areas. Because planning is an extremely important part of project management there are more planning processes used than any other processes across the knowledge areas.

Executing processes include the core processes that execute tasks such as the project plan, and team development, among other processes, such as source selection and contract administration.

The Controlling processes are concerned with keeping the project on track in terms of resources such as time and cost. Hence, these processes are connected with project performance. If significant variances are detected which may impact on the project's products, then these changes need to be picked up by the controlling processes and fed into the planning processes in order to modify the plans for the project to counteract the effects to the project.

Closing processes are concerned with closing each phase of the project as well as closing the whole project both in terms of the administrative closure, i.e., filing project documentation and records, and making sure that the products produced by the project are of a satisfactory standard and quality to the customer.

The Nine Project Management Knowledge Areas

Each project management knowledge area is discussed below together with the processes that are contained within them.

Project Integration Management

Project Integration Management is concerned with ensuring that the project is properly coordinated and contains the processes of Project Plan Development, Project Plan Execution, and Overall Change Control. These three processes both interact with each other and processes in other knowledge areas.

Project Scope Management

Project Scope Management is concerned with ensuring that the project includes all the work required in order for the successful completion of the project. This knowledge area, contains five processes being Initiation, Scope Planning, Scope Definition, Scope Verification, and Scope Change Control. As with the processes in the Project Integration Management knowledge area the processes in this knowledge area will also interact with other processes in other knowledge areas.

The Initiation process is concerned with the acknowledging that a new project exists or that an existing project should continue to its next phase.

The Scope Planning process is concerned with the development of the scope statement that will be used as guide for determining the future direction and decisions regarding the project.

The Scope Definition process is concerned with dividing the major project tasks into smaller components. Dividing the major project tasks into smaller components creates a more manageable project and allows resources, in terms of time and cost, to be more accurately predicted as resources are being estimated for smaller chunks of work rather than the whole project.

The Scope Verification process is concerned with the acceptance of the project scope by the project's customers. Products produced by the project are reviewed in order to ensure that the products have been completed correctly and properly.

The Scope Change Control process is concerned with changes to the project's scope. When a scope change request occurs, this process goes through a cycle of checking the scope change in order to determine if the scope change is beneficial to the overall project and to manage that change, if and when a scope change does occur.

Project Time Management

Project Time Management is concerned with managing the timings of the project to ensure that the project is completed on time. This knowledge area contains five processes, which interact with other processes in other knowledge areas. The five processes are Activity Definition, Activity Sequencing, Activity Duration Estimating, Schedule Development, and Schedule Control.

The Activity Definition process is concerned with identifying and documenting the activities that need to be completed in order to complete the overall project deliverables.

The Activity Sequencing process is concerned with ordering activities in sequence in order to complete activities in such a manner as to result in the completion of the project and its deliverables. Any inter-dependencies between activities will also need to be taken into consideration when sequencing activities.

The Activity Duration Estimating process is concerned with estimating the amount of time in work periods that it takes to complete each individual activity. The person who has the most expertise with an individual activity should make the time estimate of how long that activity will take to complete in work periods.

The Schedule Development process is concerned with estimating the start and finish dates of the project's individual activities. The start and finish dates need to be as realistic as possible to ensure that overall project can be completed on schedule.

The Schedule Control process is concerned with changes to the schedule, and contains tools and techniques to manage the changes to the schedule. This Schedule Control process links to and integrates with the Overall Change Control process.

Project Cost Management

Project Cost Management is concerned with the cost of resources to complete a project as well as ensuring that a project is completed within the approved budget. This knowledge area contains four processes that both interact with each other and with other processes in other knowledge areas. The four processes that the Project Cost Management knowledge area contains are Resource Planning, Cost Estimating, Cost Budgeting, and Cost Control.

The Resource Planning process is concerned with determining the physical resources, and the amounts of physical resources, such as people, equipment and materials that are required to complete the project. The Resource Planning process needs to be undertaken in conjunction with the Cost Estimating process.

The Cost Estimating process is concerned with estimating the costs of resources needed to complete the project. The resources that the cost is based on will have been identified in the Resource Planning process.

During the Cost Estimating process, consideration should be given to different costing options.

The Cost Budgeting process is concerned with assigning the cost estimates to individual tasks in the project. Therefore, each separate task within the project will have a budget assigned to it.

The Cost Control process is concerned with controlling the costs of the project. If the project costs do change, then this process is responsible for assessing whether the benefits to the project from the resulting change is justified by the added cost impact as well as managing the changes in cost.

Project Quality Management

Project Quality Management is concerned with the processes required to ensure that the products produced by the project will meet the customer expectations and requirements for which the products are intended. Quality and Quality Management is a large topic that can be approached using different methods such as the ISO (International Organization for Standardization) 9000 and 10000 series of standards and guidelines, as well as other approaches such as Total Quality Management (TQM), among others. The Project Quality Management knowledge area contains three processes being Quality Planning, Quality Assurance, and Quality Control. As with other processes, these processes interact with each other.

The Quality Planning process is concerned with identifying the standard of quality needed for the products produced by a project. The Quality Planning process is closely linked with other planning processes in other knowledge areas and needs to be performed in correlation with the other planning processes.

The Quality Assurance process is concerned with the activities needed to ensure that the products produced by the project will meet the requirements of the defined quality standards. The Quality Assurance process needs to be performed constantly throughout the project, evaluating products as they are produced.

The Quality Control process is concerned with monitoring the products produced by the project to determine whether the products meet the quality standards defined. As with the Quality Assurance process the Quality Control process needs to be performed constantly throughout the project, evaluating products as they are produced.

Project Human Resource Management

Project Human Resource Management is concerned with the effective use of all people connected with the project, which includes the project team, stakeholders, sponsors, customers, individual contributors such as consultants, and any other people connected with the project. The Project Human Resource Management knowledge area contains three processes, which are Organization Planning, Staff Acquisition, and Team Development. Like all other processes in other knowledge areas the processes in the Project Human Resource Management knowledge area interact with other processes in other knowledge areas.

The Organizational Planning process is concerned with identifying and documenting project roles and responsibilities, as well as setting up reporting structures and relationships. The Organizational Planning process is closely linked to and interacts with other planning processes in other knowledge areas.

The Staff Acquisition process is concerned with assigning the human resources needed to the project. Human resources that can be both individual people and groups of people are assigned to specific areas of the project by the project management team.

The Team Development process is concerned with both developing and enhancing the operation of the project team as well as developing and enhancing the ability of the project's stakeholders to contribute to the project. Getting a team to collaborate and work together is one of the key critical factors in the success of any project.

Project Communications Management

Project Communications Management is concerned with communication between all people and groups of people both in the project and connected to the project. The processes involved in Project Communications Management occur multiple times, in a cyclic fashion throughout the project lifecycle. In order for the project to have a greater chance of success and the communications to be effective everyone involved in the project must understand the methods and protocols used for communicating. The Project Communications Management knowledge area contains three other processes, which are Communications Planning, Information Distribution, and Performance Reporting. These processes interact with other processes in other knowledge areas as is generally applicable to the processes in every knowledge area.

The Communications Planning process is concerned with the identifying communications needs of the stakeholders in the project, and determining which stakeholders need what information and when. This process is a cyclic process, which needs to be constantly reviewed throughout the project lifecycle in order to make sure that the method for communicating with stakeholders is working, and the stakeholders are receiving the information they require when they require it. The Communications Planning process integrates and is linked to other planning processes in other knowledge areas.

The Information Distribution process is concerned with getting the information available to project stakeholders within time constraints, i.e., the time available. This process includes the implementation of a communications management plan and also manages ad hoc and one-off requests for information from stakeholders.

The Performance Reporting process is concerned with reporting the project's performance in terms of how resources are being used to achieve the project's aims and objectives. The performance report should provide information on the status and progress of a project, giving a snapshot of what has currently been achieved by the project, and the products and tasks completed. The performance report also needs to provide project-forecasting information, such as predicting the status of future projects and their progress.

The Administrative Closure process is concerned with properly closing down the project in an orderly consistent fashion, documenting project results and archiving project records. The Administrative Closure process needs to be performed after every phase of the project as well as being completed at the end of project, regardless of whether the project completed successfully or was terminated early.

Project Risk Management

Project Risk Management is concerned with identifying, analyzing, and responding to any and all risks that the project may encounter. Whenever a project of any size is undertaken, regardless of how well the project is planned there will always be an element of risk as the outcome of the project is yet unknown. The Project Risk Management knowledge area is concerned with both managing and controlling the element of risk in a project, and includes four processes to accomplish the Project Risk Management. These processes are Risk Identification, Risk Quantification, Risk Response Development, and Risk Response Control.

The Risk Identification process is concerned with identifying and documenting the risks connected to the project. This is a cyclic process that needs to be performed throughout the project's lifecycle. Both internal and external risks need to be identified as well as their effect on the project. Internal risks are events that occur within the project and project team, e.g., staff leaving, products not being completed on time, or products not being completed within budget, etc. External risks are events that occur outside the project, such as shifts in markets or changes of government policy that could affect the project.

The Risk Quantification process is concerned with evaluating risks and the implications that the risks have on both individual components of the project and the overall project. The process of evaluating risks also determines what actions are necessary to counteract the risks. The Risk Quantification process essentially follows on from the previous process Risk Identification.

The Risk Response Development process is concerned with responding to risks encountered in the project. Responses to risks or threats to the project fall into one of three categories: avoidance, mitigation, and acceptance. Avoidance of risks involves trying to eliminate the cause of a risk or threat, thereby avoiding the risk altogether, although commonly it is possible to reduce part of the risk but not the whole risk. Mitigation of risks involves reducing the financial impact of risks by reducing the probability of that particular risk occurring. An example of mitigation includes using proven technology instead of unproven technology. Acceptance has the approach of accepting the consequences of a risk and then deciding upon either an active or passive approach. An active approach would be the development of a contingency plan to counteract the effect of the risk, whereas a passive approach would be accepting the result of a lower profit should some of the project activities overrun.

The Risk Response Control process is concerned with implementing the risk management plan in response to risks that have been identified throughout the project. The processes of identifying risks, quantifying risks, and responding to risks is a cycle that occurs time and time again throughout the life of a project, as even the most thorough and comprehensive project plan will experience changes and risks.

Project Procurement Management

Project Procurement Management is concerned with acquiring goods and services needed for the project from sources that are external to the organization that is undertaking the project. The Project Procurement Management knowledge area discusses procurement from the perspective of a buyer in a buyer–seller relationship; hence, the buyer is the customer and is the key stakeholder for the seller. The seller is the organization that is undertaking the project. The Project Procurement Management knowledge area contains six processes, which are Procurement Planning, Solicitation Planning, Solicitation, Source Selection, Contract Administration, and Contract Close-out.

The Procurement Planning process is concerned with identifying those particular parts and activities in the project that can be best met by sourcing products and services from outside the project organization. The process is concerned with whether it necessary to procure products or services externally and if so, how much needs to be produced and when it needs to be procured.

The Solicitation Planning process is concerned with the preparation of documents needed to support the external procurement of goods and services to the project.

The Solicitation process is concerned with obtaining bids and proposals from prospective sellers as to how they can best meet the needs of the project that have been identified by the Procurement Planning process.

The Source Selection process is concerned with evaluating the bids and proposals from prospective sellers and selecting a particular seller. During the evaluation process a number of criteria will need to be considered such as price. Although the price of a seller's product may be the primary determining factor, the lowest price could be a false economy if the seller is not able to complete the delivery of the product in to the timescale dictated by the project; hence all aspects of a bid or proposal need to be considered before choosing a particular seller's product.

The Contract Administration process is concerned with ensuring that the seller's products and performance meets contractual requirements; hence, this process administers the contractual relationships between the buyer, the project organizations, and the seller, the organization supplying goods or services to the project organization.

The Contract Close-Out process is concerned with ensuring that all work has been completed to a satisfactory standard as well as ensuring that the records concerning the seller's completed goods and services have been updated to reflect the final results of the activities and that the records have been archived.

Starting the EDRMS Project

After deciding the project-management methodology that you will use to implement the EDRMS solution, the organization can set about starting up the project. However, before starting the project it is very important to have the right people on side. Having the right people on side can mean the difference between the project succeeding or failing.

It is of the utmost importance to have a project sponsor. This should be somebody at a senior management level within the organization, who will act as the project's champion and promote the project throughout the organization from the top downwards. This person should sit on the project board and will have significant inputs into the project on a business level.

Good working relationships are also needed with project managers, business analysts, IT developers, and IT support, as well as key users in the departments or sections of the organization where the EDRMS will first be implemented.

The project manager or consultant(s) responsible for implementing the EDRMS will need to have very good organizational and people skills since they would more often than not be working within the IT or operations section of the organization, while implementing the EDRMS in another section of the organization.

The successful implementation of an EDRMS solution is not just about selecting the correct hardware and software platforms. But just as important, if not, more important, is the need to get a unified commitment to the system from the top down from senior management.

The most critical area is that of getting different organizational departments communicating and talking to each other on a face-to-face level.

Getting the Right Team Together

Once the project board or the project sponsor is in place you can then think about getting the right team of people together to successfully implement EDRMS. You would need a project manager, a business analyst, IT trainers, and IT support personnel to support the implementation of the system and if the system is being developed in-house, IT development staff.

The team would also need access to a legal advisor, somebody with knowledge regarding the implications of storing electronic copies of legal documents and someone with knowledge regarding storing documents and records in connection with the laws of the country where the system is being implemented, laws such as Freedom of Information, Privacy and Data Protection issues, especially concerning privacy issues around citizen information.

While the system is being implemented, it is important to have a team of IT trainers to train employees and staff in the use of the system. The trainers should be on hand during working hours to generally help and facilitate the change to EDRMS. IT support should also be on hand during working hours and also out of working hours to ensure the system runs smoothly on a technical level.

The exact size of the team, in terms of business analysts, IT support personnel, IT developers, or how many IT trainers are required would entirely depend on the size of the organization. It is very important to make sure that adequate human resources are in place, to ensure that the system is supported throughout the implementation, to facilitate the change program, and to help the organization make the change to electronic documents and records that much smoother.

Chapter 13

The Business Case

The Business Case is one of the most important documents of the project as it provides justification for the project's very existence. The Business Case should illustrate the advantages the organization can achieve by implementing an EDRMS solution. These advantages need be presented as tangible and intangible benefits.

Tangible benefits are the hard gains that are made by implementing an EDRMS solution such as saving costs, saving floor space, productivity gains, and competitive advantages. Tangible benefits are the benefits that actually save the organization money and, hence, appear in the organization's accounts.

Intangible benefits are those benefits that cannot be quantified in terms of monetary gain, as is the case with tangible benefits. Intangible benefits include centralized storage of information and records, compliance with record-keeping laws and compliance with standards, improved customer service by way of increased efficiency in terms of time saved by staff accessing documents and records, improved management of information, and full disaster recovery for the organization's information, documents, and records.

Although the intangible benefits cannot be quantified in terms of monetary gain, these often have a significant impact on the organization and help to increase productivity as a whole, as well as providing additional benefits such as disaster recovery and centralized storage of documents and records, leading to improved management of information within the organization, ultimately leading to a more efficient organization overall. Therefore, intangible benefits are just as important in the business as the tangible benefits.

The business case has to sell the project to the decision makers in the organization and has to provide justification for the project in terms of the tangible and intangible benefits gained as well as the costs of the project and the cost benefits over the medium to long term.

The tangible benefits are:

- Saving costs
- Saving floor space
- Productivity gains
- Competitive advantages

Saving Costs

Implementing an EDRMS solution results in the organization's paperwork (in terms of files and folders that were located in filing rooms and filing cabinets) being scanned into the system and held electronically; hence, the organization will save money on the furniture costs of cabinets, files, folders, and some stationary costs.

Saving Floor Space

Floor space that was used to house the filing rooms, filing cabinets, files and folders will also be saved, allowing the space to be used for other purposes and potentially saving the organization's either moving to larger premises or purchasing or renting additional floor space. With regards to saving the organization from moving to larger premises or purchasing or renting additional floor space, these savings can be quite significant.

If the implementation of the EDRMS solution also leads to increased productivity gains, then floor space can also be saved with regard to a possible reduction in employing and housing staff.

Productivity Gains

Enabling the organization's staff and allowing them to access the organization's information (documents and records) in an electronic format while seated at their desks in front of their PCs within a matter of seconds or at most minutes will definitely result in productivity gains and increased efficiency over having to physically locate documents or records from a filing room.

The increased efficiency of the EDRMS solution allows existing staff to process more, faster, and ultimately leads to an increase in productivity, i.e., more work being completed using the same number of staff. This also means that the organization would not have to employ more staff to complete a greater amount of work, which leads to significant cost savings for the organization, not just in terms of employee costs, but also in terms of associated floor space to locate those employees as well as furniture costs and computer costs.

Competitive Advantages

The implementation of an EDRMS solution will lead to increased efficiency within the organization, therefore leading to improved customer satisfaction. This, in turn, has the effect of helping the organization to retain existing customers and acquire new customers. Hence, the implementation of the EDRMS solution has given the organization a competitive advantage over its competitors.

Intangible benefits are:

- Centralized storage of information
- Management of information
- Compliance with record keeping laws and standards
- Improved customer services
- Improved staff morale
- Encouraging team working
- More efficient business processes
- Full disaster recovery

Centralized Storage of Information

The implementation of an EDRMS solution will allow the organization to store its information (documents and records) in a central location, accessible via a central server, and the information will be accessible from anywhere within the organization. In the case of organizations that have multiple sites, this also has the benefit of allowing staff access to information that previously was not held at their site.

By storing information in a central location, as with an EDRMS solution, the organization becomes more efficient with staff saving time while searching for and retrieving documents. This time saving translates into money saved for the organization, but as you cannot put a firm figure on it, it has been listed here as an intangible benefit. Time saved within the organization also has the effect of increasing productivity as well as improving customer satisfaction.

Management of Information

The implementation of the EDRMS solution leads to better management of information because information is now held in a central location. This means the organization knows where all its information is at any one time and can account for all its information.

Compliance with Record Keeping Laws and Standards

Compliance with record keeping laws and regulatory standards is one of the biggest driving factors for organizations implementing EDRMS. There are currently many laws that require organizations to be accountable for and retain records for accounting purposes, such as the Sarbanes–Oxley Act. The Freedom of Information Act is also another compelling reason for organizations to implement an EDRMS solution.

Organizations must be accountable for all the information they retain regarding their business interactions, whether these business interactions concern individuals, businesses, accounts, sales, products, licensing or whatever. By implementing a compliant EDRMS solution for their business sector, organizations can ensure they are remaining compliant with laws and regulatory standards.

Improved Customer Service

The successful implementation of an EDRMS solution ultimately results in improved customer service gained through increased efficiency within the organization. Increased efficiency is achieved through many different aspects of the EDRMS implementation, such as quicker and easier access to documents and records, more efficient business processes and increased staff morale. Hence, the increased efficiency in turn leads to improved customer service.

Improved Staff Morale

Improved staff morale is the result of staff being able to access documents and records in a much easier and quicker fashion, not having to physically look for documents in filing rooms and filing cabinets. Higher staff morale results in happier workers, and happier workers are more productive workers.

More Efficient Business Processes

Streamlined and more efficient business processes are achieved with the implementation of EDRMS. The vast majority of an organization's business processes use documents that are an integral part of the business process. If documents can be handled electronically, this will result in more efficient handling of documents. Also, if workflow is incorporated with the EDRMS solution and business processes are reengineered using workflow process maps, this also makes business processes more efficient since the documents and records do not have to be manually transferred across the organization.

Encouraging Team Working

Improved staff morale, as well as more efficient business processes, also encourages team working, which in turn leads to increased efficiency within the organization.

Full Disaster Recovery

The implementation of an EDRMS solution means that the organization's information, their documents and records are held in a central location in a networked storage solution permitting the data to be backed up and allowing for the information to be restored in the event of a disaster. Without the implementation of an EDRMS, this would not be the case because the organization's documents and records would be located in filing cabinets and filing rooms as paper files. Hence, in the event of a fire or other catastrophe that resulted in the organization's building becoming inaccessible, this information would be lost forever. However, with the implementation of EDRMS, a backup routine involving secure off-site locations for disaster recovery would also be established as part of the computer hardware requirements that would enable information to be recovered in the event of a major disaster occurring.

The Link between Tangible Benefits and Intangible Benefits

The implementation of an EDRMS solution does not produce a range of single benefits in isolation of each other, whether tangible or intangible benefits, but instead produces a range of benefits. All these benefits, both tangible and intangible are interlinked and feed off each other and are complimented by each other. For example, gains in productivity lead to saving costs as well as saving floor space, which also lead into saving costs. Saving costs also gives the organization a competitive advantage. Productivity gains, which are one of the results of more efficient business processes, lead to improved customer service and improved customer satisfaction. Hence, all these benefits are interlinked and feed off each other.

Costs of the Project

There are many costs associated with implementing an EDRMS solution, which can be grouped into different areas enabling a cost breakdown. Initially the cost of implementing an EDRMS solution across the organization would outweigh any savings made. However, over a period of time, e.g., two to three years, the organization would hit a breakeven point where the cost of the project equals the savings made, and after this time the organization is actually saving money as a direct result of the implementation of the EDRMS solution. The point at which the organization breaks even with the cost of the project versus savings made is known as the Return on Investment (ROI). The quicker the ROI is for the organization, the more appealing it is to implement an EDRMS solution.

The costs associated with implementing an EDRMS solution can be broken down in following specific areas:

- Project Management
- Information Gathering and Analysis
- The Feasibility Study
- The Business Case
- The Functional Requirements
- The Technical Specification
- Procuring an EDRMS software solution
- IT hardware costs
- Implementation costs
- Training costs
- Support costs
- Maintenance costs

Project Management

Setting up the project initially involves putting a project manager and business analysts in place. If the organization is planning to use in-house staff, then costs will be less than externally recruiting. However, the cost of using the project manager and business analysts need to be factored into the overall costs. Consideration needs to be given not just to the cost of using these staff but also to any travel expenses and equipment that may be needed during the course of the project.

Information Gathering and Analysis

The information gathering and analysis activities are a critical stage during the time of the project as the feasibility study, business case, functional requirements, and technical specification documents depend to a large extent on the information gathered during this stage.

Costs for information gathering and analysis activities include business analysts. Again, if the organization is using in-house business analysts, then these costs will be significantly reduced, compared to recruiting external business consultants. However, as with project management costs, factors such as travel expenses and equipment required to complete the information gathering and analysis exercise need to be factored in to the overall cost of this stage.

The information gathering and analysis stage of the project would start at the beginning of the project before the feasibility study is produced and normally run until the technical specification document has been produced, hence this process does not start and stop before the feasibility study is produced. Instead, it is an on-going process that aids the production of all documents, up to and including the technical specification.

The Feasibility Study

The feasibility study is the document that determines if it is viable to implement an EDRMS solution within the organization. This document is largely a result of the previous exercise, information gathering, and analysis. This document needs to be written and signed off by the project manager, and the cost of this has to be calculated for this stage of the overall project.

The Business Case

The business case is a comprehensive document and one of the most important documents of the project as the business case provides the justification for the project's very existence. Hence, this book has dedicated a whole chapter to the Business Case.

As with the feasibility study, this document has to be produced and signed off by the project manager before it goes before the decision makers in the organization. Hence, the cost of developing and writing the business plan needs to be determined for this stage as well as being factored into the overall cost of the project.

The Functional Requirements

The Functional Requirements document defines what the EDRMS solution needs to accomplish within the organization on a functional level. This document is produced using the information gathering and analysis that has been carried out within the organization. Again, the time taken and cost of writing this document needs to be accounted for in the overall project budget.

The Technical Specification

The Technical Specification document defines the technical architecture of the EDRMS solution in terms of folder structure, document types, workflow process maps, records retention and disposal rules, and security and access, among other technical details. This document is produced using the information gathering and analysis conducted within the organization and follows on from the functional requirements document. Again, the cost of developing and writing this document needs to be factored into the overall project spend.

Procuring an EDRMS Software Solution

The procurement of an EDRMS software solution is one of the largest costs of the project. The software is normally priced on per server, per user, or concurrent user cost basis. Negotiating with the software suppliers on costs can often mean savings to the organization, as the software vendors generally have flexibility with regards to their product's list price.

IT Hardware Costs

Implementing an EDRMS solution will result in new IT hardware being purchased in terms of scanners, servers, and network storage solutions, among other hardware. The cost of the new hardware has to be factored into the overall project costs.

Implementation Costs

Costs associated with the implementation phase of the EDRMS project include consultancy from the EDRMS software supplier and the costs associated with developing and implementing the change program, as well as any change management consultancy that has been purchased externally.

Suppliers will normally quote their consultancy costs on a daily rate and should be able to give a fairly accurate estimate for installation costs. For other activities, such as developing workflows and business process reengineering activities it may be harder for the suppliers to give accurate estimates, and some suppliers may not give any. Allowance has to be made in the project budget for all the costs associated with the implementation such as installation costs, consultancy day rate costs for other activities such as workflow and business process reengineering activities, travel expenses and any other equipment needed for the implementation phase.

Training Costs

During the implementation phase of the project, as well as after the implementation phase has been completed, users in the organization need to be trained in the use of the new system. For organizations with large numbers of staff, the training costs to train all staff can be considerable. The training costs can be reduced by training only key users in the use of the system, and then allowing these key users to train other staff in the organization. However, whichever method is used to train staff, the cost must still be factored into the overall project cost.

IT Support Costs

From the start of the implementation phase, the EDRMS solution will need to be supported, both in terms of the hardware the system uses, such as servers, networked storage space, and scanners, as well as the software and operational support needed for users within the organization.

If the organization has enough spare IT Support capacity to cope with the expected demand in support for the EDRMS solution, then there will not be any extra costs associated with the implementation and on-going support of the system. However, if the organization has to recruit extra staff to cope with the demand on IT Support, then these costs have to be factored into the overall project cost.

It is also important to note that IT Support personnel will also need to receive sufficient training at a level that gives them the necessary knowledge in order to maintain and administer the system. This training will normally be provided by the EDRMS software vendor and is normally charged for by the day.

Maintenance Costs

Suppliers of EDRMS software solutions charge an annual fee for maintenance of their software. Maintenance normally covers product support, troubleshooting, and bug fixing. Maintenance costs vary with suppliers. However, the cost of maintenance will need to be factored into the overall project cost.

Stages Running in Parallel

During the stages of the project, such as information gathering and analysis, the feasibility study, and the business case, it is possible and even advantageous to run these processes in parallel. For example, the information gathering and analysis process could run while the feasibility study and business case documents are being produced, and in turn the information gathering and analysis process would be a much longer process running alongside other stages such as developing the functional requirements and developing the technical specification. At the same time, the development of the functional requirements document and technical specification document could happen together in parallel with information gathering and analysis exercises still being carried out where required.

Financial Benefits of the Project

The financial benefits of implementing the EDRMS solution need to be presented to the decision makers in the organization. This section of the business case should present the cost of implementing the EDRMS solution, measured against the ROI, and should include the following explanations:

- Why the organization should invest in an EDRMS solution
- The costs of investing in the EDRMS solution broken down as separate costs of the project
- When the organization will start seeing a ROI
- The savings that will result over the project life
- The tangible and intangible benefits that will result from the implementation of the EDRMS solution

The financial benefits of the project need to include both optimistic and pessimistic project costs and project savings forecasts. This section of the business case has to sell the EDRMS project to the decision makers of the organization in monetary terms, ideally showing a saving of costs over the medium to long term. If the saving in costs over this period is not substantial then the business case will need to rely on selling the project using intangible benefits, and emphasizing that the advantages of the intangible benefits outweigh the estimated cost of the project. The business case needs to focus on the strongest points contained within it in order to effectively sell the project.

Chapter 14

The Functional Requirements

The functional requirements document specifies the functionality required of an EDRMS solution and the development of this document normally takes place after the information gathering and analysis stage has already started. However, during the development of the functional requirements document there will be on-going information gathering and analysis for the main purpose of further defining and clarifying the exact functional requirements needed by the organization.

As the functional requirements document specifies what the EDRMS solution needs to be able to do on a functional level, this document is of key importance in the procurement of a prospective solution, as the functionality of any prospective solution can be checked against the functional requirements, and if a prospective solution does not have the functionality required by the organization that particular solution can be ruled out. Hence, the functional requirements document becomes the benchmark by which EDRMS functionality is judged.

Chapter 2 presented four different standards, listed below:

- ISO 15489, an International Standard for the Management of Records
- MOREQ — Model Requirements for the Management of Electronic Records
- DoD 5015.2 — Design Criteria Standard for Electronic Records Management Software Applications
- TNA 2002 — The National Archives (United Kingdom)

The above standards all detail what is functionally required of an EDRMS solution in order for a particular vendor's product to comply with the standards issued by the respective standards bodies. However, individual organizations will require their prospective EDRMS solutions to conform to their own specific requirements. Hence, it therefore becomes important that any organization that is in the process of procuring an EDRMS solution investigates what their own specific requirements for that solution are and develop their own functional requirements document.

The four standards guides above can and should be used as reference documents in the development of the organization's functional requirements document. The rest of this chapter discusses the topics that should be included in a functional requirements document, which can be used as a baseline template for developing the organization's specific functional requirements. However, the organization must also consider their own specific requirements.

Folder Structure

In defining the functional requirements of the EDRMS folder structure you will need to specify the functionality connected to folder structures. For example, if the organization planned to implement a hybrid folder structure utilizing the four approaches discussed in Chapter 5, Creating the Folder Structure, then in determining the functional requirements for the folder structure, the requirement could be worded as follows:

> The EDRMS must be able to support a hierarchical folder structure that is able to support five levels of folders in a hierarchical fashion.

> The EDRMS folder structure must be able to be set up and maintained, including being modified by authorized administrative users.

Note that both the statements above specify the requirements of the EDRMS folder structure in that the folder structure must be hierarchical and that the system must also allow authorized administrative users to set up, maintain, and modify the structure. Hence, an EDRMS solution that complies with both the functional requirements specified above will allow the organization to set up and maintain a folder structure using the hybrid approach discussed in Chapter 5, Creating the Folder Structure.

Document Types and Metadata

When defining the functional requirements for document types and metadata, the vast majority of organizations will require a flexible approach to the design of document types as well as metadata. Therefore, the functional requirements statements concerning document types and meta-data can be worded as follows:

> The EDRMS must be able to support the creation of an infinite number of document types.
>
> The EDRMS must be able to support the creation of an infinite number of metadata fields, and each metadata field must allow both preselected values and values entered by users.
>
> The EDRMS must allow an authorized administrative user to assign any and all metadata fields to all and any document types.
>
> The EDRMS must allow an authorized administrative user to update and maintain all and any document types created.
>
> The EDRMS must allow an authorized administrative user to update and maintain all and any metadata fields created, as well as their predetermined values where they exist.

All five statements above specify that the EDRMS solution will need to have a flexible approach to creation and maintenance of document types and metadata. This will allow administrative users of the system the ability to create document types with associated metadata as per the organization's requirements, an example of which has been discussed in Chapter 4, Creating Electronic Document Types.

Search and Retrieval

The functional requirements concerning searching and retrieval mechanisms for the EDRMS solution should include definitions for both basic and advanced searches, as well as specifying being able to search on both document and record content using an OCR enabled search. Hence, the functional requirements for search and retrieval should include statements such as:

> All EDRMS search facilities must be able to search both metadata field values and the main body content of all documents and records.
>
> The EDRMS search facility must include a basic search that allows users of the basic search to select how they wish to search for documents using either "any of the words," "all of the words," or "exact phrase" options. The basic search must default to the "any of the words" option.
>
> The EDRMS search facility must include an advanced search facility that can automatically pick up all metadata fields from any and all document types.

> The EDRMS Advanced search must allow users to construct complex search criteria statements using Boolean operators AND, OR, and NOT with any or all the metadata fields of the document type being searched for.

> The EDRMS Advanced search must allow users to search for documents and records by specifying date ranges either with or without an accompanying search criterion, using the metadata fields of the document type being searched for.

The five functional requirements statements made above specify that the EDRMS will need to provide search and retrieval functionality in accordance with the functionality discussed for both basic and advanced search mechanisms as in Chapter 6, Search and Retrieval.

Document Management

In this section of the functional requirements you will be defining the document management needs of the organization in terms of the file types, i.e., type of files that can be stored within the system, version control, check-in and check-out procedures, and any other specific document management functionality as needed by the organization. In order to define the functional requirements for document management, the following statements can be included in the functional requirements document.

> The EDRMS must be able to store any and all files of any size and file types, including but not limited to .doc, .xls, .ppt, .pdf, .bmp, and .txt.

> The EDRMS must allow an authorized administrative user to specify additional file types that the EDRMS can store.

> The EDRMS must allow an authorized administrative user to specify which file types can be stored in which folders, on a per folder level.

> The EDRMS must support version control of all documents, and must retain previous versions of documents.

> The EDRMS must support check-in and check-out functionality allowing documents and files to be checked out, and when checked out, the documents or files must be locked in read-only mode to any other user that requests a copy of the checked-out document or file.

The five statements above define what is required for basic document management functionality. The approach taken to storing documents and files needs to be flexible as the organization's needs will change over time and as new file formats come out.

Records Management

Records Management requirements will consist of retention and archiving of records as well as deletion guidelines and methods used for deleting records once the time for the records to be retained has expired. An off-line storage facility for records that no longer have to be retained on-line also needs to be specified. The following statements can be used to define the records management functional requirements for an organization. The EDRMS must:

> Authorize an administrative user to set up and maintain retention rules, specified as the period in time that a particular document type must be retained and kept accessible by the system
>
> Support the archiving of records, by either completely destroying the records or moving the records to off-line storage media once the retention period comes to an end
>
> Allow an authorized administrative user to archive both individual records and groups of records at any time
>
> Allow an authorized administrative user to archive both individual folders and groups of folders located in the folder structure hierarchy at any time
>
> Allow an authorized user to declare a document or file within the system as a record that is not able to undergo any further changes whatsoever

The five statements above define the basic records management functionality needed for most organization's records management requirements. However, the records management functionality does need to be somewhat flexible as an organization's records management requirements can change with the impact of new legislation or regulations and changes in business practices.

User Interfaces

The requirements for user interfaces will mainly depend upon whether the organization will be implementing a Web-based user interface or implementing a Windows-based user interface or a combination of both. The following statements assume that an organization will be implementing both

Web- and Windows-based user interface clients, as well as a user interface that needs to run on a mobile PDA device. The EDRMS must support:

> The use of a Web-based user interface

> The use of a Windows-based user interface

> The development of a mobile PDA-based user interface, capable of running and displaying images on a PDA/Pocket PC platform

The first two statements above simply specify that the EDRMS must support both a Web-based and Windows-based user interface; however, the third statement mentions the need for the development of a mobile PDA-based user interface.

There are currently a number of PDA operating systems platforms, some of which are Microsoft Windows-based and some are Java-based, and as it may not, at this stage during the development of the functional requirements and implementation of the EDRMS solution be known as to exactly which type of mobile device the organization intends to use, we need to employ a certain degree of flexibility in the statement of requirements that specify the need for a mobile user interface.

Mobile Working and Remote Access

The functional requirements for mobile working and remote access firstly depend upon whether the organization's implementation of EDRMS is to include mobile working and remote access features. In the following examples, we will assume that an organization is implementing its EDRMS solution with both mobile working practices and remote access requirements, which are stated in the following functional requirements statements:

> The EDRMS must support access via the organization's VPN (Virtual Private Network) to provide mobile working and remote access.

> The EDRMS must support a user interface that can be used on a PDA device or any such device used for mobile working and remote access.

The first statement above specifies that the system must provide access via the organization's VPN. However, the second statement overlaps into the user interface functional requirements. This is because of the link between devices (PDAs are used both for mobile working and remote access) and also the need for PDA devices to have their own custom user interface due to the limitations of the operating system and screen size.

Security and Access

EDRMS solutions need to incorporate security and access functionality, allowing systems administrators to determine which users or groups of users can access which files (documents or records) or groups of files, which is normally achieved by applying security settings to sections of the hierarchical folder structure. The exact security and access requirements will entirely depend upon the organization's needs. However, listed below are statements that will allow an organization to implement user- and group-based security as determined by the organization's own specific requirements. The EDRMS must allow an authorized administrative user to:

> Create and maintain individual users of the system
>
> Create and maintain user groups of the system
>
> Assign security and access permissions to individual users and user groups
>
> Assign security and access permissions to individual documents and records as well as groups of documents and records
>
> Assign security and access permissions to individual folders as well as groups of folders in the folder structure
>
> Grant and deny access to the entire system or sections of the system for both individual users and groups of users

The statements above specify that systems administrators need to have the functionality in order to create users and groups of users, assign security and access permissions to those users, as well as specifying security and access permissions at both the individual file (documents and records) level, and folder level. The requirements also state administrators must have the ability to grant and deny access to system functionality for certain users and groups of users, i.e., only certain users will have the authority to create new document types or modify the folder structure.

Auditing

Auditing facilities allow authorized users to access the history of documents and records, allowing them to view which documents have been changed and when, and in the case of records when they were archived as records, as shown by the functional requirements statement below.

> The EDRMS must allow an authorized administrative user access the history of both documents and records as audit trails.

Reporting

The functional requirements for reporting most commonly center on the production of statistical analysis regarding the use of the system, in terms of document types accessed and searches performed. The system needs to have a flexible approach to the design of searching facilities, allowing authorized administrative users the ability to design bespoke reports as required. Thus, the statements following address the basic reporting facilities needed by most organizations.

> The EDRMS must allow an authorized administrative user to create and maintain bespoke reports on documents, records, and individual document types and search facilities.
>
> The EDRMS must allow an authorized administrative user the facility to produce statistical reports on the usage of the system in terms of number of users, amounts of documents and records accessed, and access times for documents and records.

Administration

The administrative features of an EDRMS solution are mainly concerned with maintaining the system as well as making changes to the system as dictated by the organization's requirements. Hence, an authorized administrative user will need the ability to modify and create new document types, update the folder structure, delete documents and records, and so forth. The statements following detail the basic functional administrative requirements needed in order to maintain an EDRMS solution. The EDRMS must allow an authorized administrative user to:

> Create new document types and maintain existing document types
>
> Create and maintain the folder structure
>
> Delete documents and records
>
> Create and maintain retention schedules
>
> Back up both sections of the system and entire system

Compliance with Standards

Complying with the various laws and regulations concerning documents and, most important, records and citizen data is a complicated matter, which differs depending upon the country the organization operates in as well as the industry sector the organization operates in. In determining some of the requirements to comply with standards we will be considering organizations based in different countries and operating within different business sectors.

For our first example, let us consider an organization that is operating within the healthcare industry in the United States. Our example healthcare organization will need to comply with the following standards, laws and regulations, as detailed by the functional requirements statements detailed as follows:

DoD 5015.2

Health Insurance Portability and Accountability Act 1996

Sarbanes–Oxley Act 2002

Freedom of Information Act

Privacy Act of 1974

For the next example, let us consider a healthcare organization, which is based in the United Kingdom. The EDRMS must comply with:

The National Archives Functional Requirements 2002 (TNA 2002)

The Freedom of Information Act 2000

The Data Protection Act 1998

Notice the difference with the laws and regulations, by comparing the healthcare organizations in the United States to the healthcare organizations in the United Kingdom.

As a minimum requirement, organizations based in the United States will need to comply with either DoD 5015.2 or ISO 15489, but as DoD 5015.2 is a set of functional requirements designed and developed in the United States, and endorsed by the National Archives and Records Administration (NARA), DoD 5015.2 is probably the better set of functional requirements for organizations in the United States to comply with.

As well as complying a records keeping standard, such as DoD 5015.2 or ISO 15489, organizations in the United States also have to comply with the Sarbanes–Oxley Act 2002, the Freedom of Information Act, and the Privacy Act. Additionally, depending upon the industry sector the organization is based in, the organization may also have to comply with other Acts such as the Health Insurance Portability and Accountability Act of 1996.

Organizations in the United Kingdom, as a minimum, need to comply with either The National Archives (TNA) 2002 functional requirements or ISO 15489 standard. Additionally, organizations in the United Kingdom, regardless of size or industry sector, must comply with both the Freedom of Information Act 2000 and the Data Protection Act 1998.

Chapter 15

The Technical Specification

The Technical Specification includes many of the same headings as the Functional Requirements document and builds upon the functional requirements document. It also needs to include detailed information such as exactly how document types and meta data should be defined, as well as how the folder structure and other sections of the EDRMS solution should be defined. Hence, the Technical Specification document is needed by the technical system's implementation staff in the setup and implementation of the EDRMS solution.

Much of work needed to produce the Technical Specification, such as defining the folder structure and creating document types, among other sections of the system, has already been detailed in Part 2, Components of EDRMS, so a large part of this chapter will simply recap and reference Part 2 of this book.

Folder Structure

Chapter 5, Creating the Folder Structure, discussed four different approaches and recommended the hybrid approach, which can be taken in creating the folder structure for an organization's EDRMS solution. Under this heading we need to provide a detailed technical specification of the folder structure so that technical systems implementators can create the folder structure specified here, within the EDRMS solution.

Document Types and Metadata

Chapter 4, Creating Electronic Document Types, discussed the approach that needs to taken in order to create electronic document types with their associated metadata paper forms using the example of the Health and Safety Report of an injury or dangerous occurrence.

This section of the Technical Specification requires a detailed technical specification of all document types, together with the document types meta-data that will be used in the system.

Search and Retrieval

Chapter 6, Search and Retrieval, discusses both basic and advanced searches, as well as being able to search the content of a document. This section of the Technical Specification requires the specification of both basic and advanced search screens and, as well, how the search results are displayed.

Document Management

The technical specifications concerning document management need to be drawn and based on the functional requirements for document management. First and foremost, the document management technical specifications need to specify the types of files that the system will manage, i.e., file types.

The technical specification for achieving both version control, together with check-in and check-out procedures, also need to be specified, together with screen mock-ups of the screens that will display different versions of documents as well as identifying which files have been checked out.

Administrative functions concerning document management, such as authorized administrative users being able to specify additional file types that the EDRMS can manage, also needs to be specified, again together with screen mock-ups showing how this functionality is to be achieved. The file types that can be stored within particular folders in the hierarchical folder structure also need to be specified here together with corresponding screen mock-ups.

Records Management

Chapter 9, Records Management Policies, discusses the subjects of retention guidelines concerning how long a time period an organization needs to keep records. The chapter also discusses different methods for handling those records once the time to retain them expires, such as moving the records to off-line storage or destroying them entirely.

This section of the Technical Specification requires that record retention guidelines are listed against all document types, together with rules for handling the records once their retention time has expired.

User Interfaces

Chapter 10, User Interfaces, Mobile Working and Remote Access, discusses both the Windows client user interface and the Web client user interface, as well as approaches that can be taken towards implementing a user interface for mobile working using devices such as PDAs.

The technical specification of the user interfaces, whether the organization plans to deploy either Web or Windows clients or both — as well as whether a "custom" user interface needs to be deployed for mobile working using a PDA device — will depend upon the organization's functional requirements. The user interfaces that are required need to be specified in this section of the Technical Specification, using screen mock-ups of the proposed user interface as well as textual explanations of how the user interfaces function.

Mobile Working and Remote Access

As well as discussing user interfaces, Chapter 10 also discusses mobile working and remote access and much of the same information as given in the section above applies here, in that the specification of the mobile working and remote access requirements depend upon what has been specified in the functional requirements.

Security and Access

In order to implement security and access permissions in the system, this section of the technical specification requires a complete list of users and user groups, together with their security and access privileges specified to enable the information to be taken form this document and implemented onto the live system.

Auditing

The auditing of documents and records allows authorized users to access the history of documents and records, thereby viewing which users have been responsible for archiving records, as well as creating and updating documents and producing audit trails.

Auditing is an important feature and is a core requirement of many compliance laws and regulations. The technical specifications for auditing requirements would need to include screen mock-ups, including the functionality of document and record history screens.

Reporting

The technical specifications for the solutions reporting functionality need to be based on the requirements for reporting as described in the functional requirements document and need to include a specific description and screen mock-ups detailing how authorized administrative users of the system will create and maintain bespoke reports on documents, records, individual document types, and search facilities.

The EDRMS solution also needs to contain a set of predefined reports that authorized administrative users can run. These predefined reports need to be based on the organization's reporting requirements but also need to cover a cross section of individual document types and reports on document and record activities, as well as predefined reports on searching facilities and how users of the EDRMS solution are using these searching facilities.

In most organizations there will also be an emphasis on producing statistical reports measuring certain sections of system activity, such as how many times a certain document or record has been viewed, total number of records in the system, etc.

All these reports need to be fully detailed in this section of the technical specification. Each report specified needs to be laid out in the technical specification, as it would appear on the screen. A full list of reports also needs to be laid out in a screen mock-up, as well as screen mock-ups detailing how users can create and maintain other bespoke reports that have not been predefined.

Administration

Administration is concerned with maintaining the system in terms of document types, folder structure, and retention schedules, among other elements of the system, once these elements of the system have been set up and the system is being used in a live production environment.

As with other sections of the technical specifications, the information required for this section of the technical specification document needs to be based upon the requirements in the functional requirements document.

The functional requirements specified five administrative functions, listed below, that the system needs to incorporate. The EDRMS must allow an authorized administrative user to:

Create new document types and maintain existing document types

Create and maintain the folder structure

Delete documents and records

Create and maintain retention schedules

Create and maintain deletion schedules

Back up both sections of the system and entire system

Each of these statements needs to be expanded upon with detailed technical specifications involving screen mock-ups and descriptions of how the functionality will be incorporated into the system. The organization will also need to consider other areas of administrative functions with the system and, if identified, incorporate these requirements firstly into the functional requirements document and then detail them in the technical specifications.

Chapter 16

EDRMS Software Platforms

There are many commercially available EDRMS solutions produced by specialist software companies who have many years experience in the document and records management arena. A lot of companies have developed and are moving towards Enterprise Content Management (ECM) Solutions.

ECM packages commonly provide an organization with a suite of business software packages covering functionality such as Document Management, Records Management, Web Content Management, Collaboration Tools, Workflow Tools, Scanning and Imaging, among other functionality. In addition to ECM offerings, many companies offer a modular approach to ECM, allowing an organization to purchase those modules that they require. For example, if an organization wanted to implement just Document Management then they would simply purchase just the Document Management component. Later the company could purchase the Records Management module. Alternatively, a company that may want to implement both Document Management and Records Management and Workflow at the same time would purchase these modules together. Other software vendors offer separate Document Management and Records Management solutions, whereas other companies offer complete EDRMS solutions in one complete package.

Choosing the "Right" (?) Software

There really is no "best" EDRMS software available, only the best package for your organization's needs and requirements. As every organization has unique needs and requirements for EDRM, selecting an individual package really depends on several different factors as well as the individual importance of each individual factor. The main factors to take into consideration are listed in Figure 16.1.

- Does the organization require Document Management functionality?
- Does the organization require Records Management functionality?
- Does the organization require Workflow functionality?
- How many users will need to access the system?
- Does the organization need to comply with legislation such as Freedom of Information, Data Protection, and Privacy matters?
- Is the organization in the private or public sector?
- Does the organization need to comply with standards such as DoD 5015.2 or TNA 2002?
- How will the organization implement the new system? Phased Implementation, Parallel Implementation, Pilot Implementation, or Direct Changeover?

Figure 16.1   Considerations in selecting EDRMS software.

Appendix A contains short summaries of the document and records management software available from most of the major vendors. These short summaries have been provided to give a general snapshot overview of commercially available products.

In addition to purchasing a commercially available solution there is also the option of developing a solution in-house if the organization has the resources available. This option is discussed in the following section.

The D.I.Y Option — In-House Development

An alternative to purchasing a commercially available off-the-shelf EDRM system is to develop a system in-house. The main advantage of developing a system in-house as opposed to buying a commercially available product is that the organization can develop and design the system to their own specific organizational needs and objectives.

The downside to developing an in-house system is that this will require both human resources, time and money, and will need to be managed as an entirely separate project in itself, separate to the implementation of the EDRMS.

At its most basic level an EDRM system is essentially a database application that manages images and the actual technology from a computer programming and software development perspective is not very complicated. *The complicated part is implementing the system in the organization.*

The cost difference between buying a commercially available system and developing a system in-house could be another reason to consider the in-house option. Let's say a medium-sized organization of around 500 users intended to purchase a commercially available EDRM system and have the system implemented by the product vendors. The added cost of purchasing the product, the user license fees, consultancy fees and maintenance contracts could well mean that it would be more cost effective to develop a system in-house.

On the other hand it may well be worth implementing a commercially available product as the product vendors could be specialists in a certain industry sector and the organization could gain from their prior knowledge and experience implementing systems in other organizations in the same sector to their own.

To sum up, there are pros and cons to both approaches, and you can't say that one approach is better than the other. It all depends on the organization's needs and what is right for the organization at that particular time.

Chapter 17

Hardware Considerations

An EDRMS solution is an enterprise solution that, once implemented and fully operational, will become critical to the organization — a mission-critical system. Careful consideration needs to be given to ensuring that the EDRMS software is hosted on a reliable, scalable, and robust hardware platform that is not susceptible to a hard drive crash or even a server crash. The system simply must be resilient enough to cope with the most catastrophic failures!

Although this book is not primarily concerned with hardware platforms or subjects like backup and disaster recovery, it is because these matters are often left aside and not properly addressed throughout many organizations, and because they are so important in the successful running of a mission-critical system such as EDRMS, a short chapter is presented here discussing these issues.

Mirroring Servers

Mirroring Servers is a technique where an identical copy — a mirror — of a main server is created and maintained, in terms of being kept up to date in the event that the main server may crash or suffer some other failure, in which case the mirrored server takes over.

Mirroring Servers is an effective method to provide fault tolerance. It does mean having a dedicated copy of a main server, in case the main server goes down. Hence, although it is effective, it is not inexpensive.

Clustering

Clustering involves connecting two or more servers together so that they may behave like a single computer. Clustering is quite a popular approach as it utilizes hardware, provides for better performance through employing load balancing, and also provides for fault tolerance.

Mirroring Servers, on the other hand, employs redundant copies of server and, hence, is a more expensive and less efficient option than clustering.

Backup Facilities

As well as having adequate procedures in place for hardware failure such as mirroring servers or clustering, it is also of the utmost importance to have adequate backup facilities to back up all data, documents and records on a daily basis. Data backup is normally carried out using tape drives, and data is backed up on a scheduled routine.

Disaster Recovery

Disaster Recovery procedures refer to the continued existence of a computer system and all its data after major catastrophe, such as an earthquake or other disaster. Disaster Recovery is a huge topic that warrants a dedicated book of its own, however it is important to build in disaster recovery procedures such as storing backups off-site whenever mission critical systems, such as EDRMS solutions are concerned.

Scanners

As scanners are also a critical component of the EDRMS hardware solution they, too, need to have adequate backup and recovery resources in place. Scanners do break down; hence, an organization should always keep spare scanning capacity, in the way of at least one spare scanner on site, and perhaps other consumable spares associated with the scanning machines. It is also possible to get maintenance contracts for scanners with specified call-out times and fixing times. Consideration should be given to either taking out a scanning maintenance contract or, if the organization has the necessary expertise on site, keeping spare scanning consumables and parts on site.

It is also advantageous to have slightly more scanning machines than you need within the organization as this will help both with periods of increased scanning and also acts to provide fault tolerance in the event that a scanner does break down.

Chapter 18

Managing the Cultural Change of EDRMS

Implementing an EDRMS solution represents an entirely new way of working for the vast majority of staff within an organization. Traditionally, the organization and its staff have been used to working with paper files and folders. When users needed to refer to a certain document or record they would obtain those documents or records from either a filing cabinet or a filing room.

Managing the cultural change that an organization goes through in implementing an EDRMS solution is absolutely critical to the success of the system. This cannot be stressed enough.

In the vast majority of cases where an EDRMS solution has not delivered or lived up to promises made, it is often the case that not enough attention has been paid to the cultural change aspects of radically altering the way in which the staff of an organization works.

Through the implementation of EDRMS, an organization is fundamentally from the inside out changing the way and the method in which employees both retain and work with information — information being documents and records. If the staff of the organization is resistant to the implementation of EDRMS then it will not want to work with the new system, but is essentially forced to work with a new system, which it doesn't like and doesn't want. This, in turn, can lead to lower staff morale, which in turn has the knock on effect of lower productivity, more days off, more staff going sick, and so forth. In extreme cases, nonadherence to the cultural changes involved with the implementation of new computer systems has led to major breakdowns in organizations and severe backlogs within the organization, ultimately resulting in very poor productivity and customer service.

This chapter discusses the aspects and fundamentals of change management, both in terms of implementing a change management program and managing the cultural change within an organization during and after the implementation of EDRMS.

What Is Change Management?

Change Management refers to the processes and associated actions and tasks required in order to manage any type of change that occurs within an organization. Change Management is concerned with the impact of new ways of working within organizations and the effect that those new ways of working have on the individuals that make up the organization, the organization's staff.

Change Management is a not a discrete subject and is a discipline that contains elements of many other subjects, where these individual subjects are concerned with the impact of change. Change Management contains elements of psychology, sociology, economics, business administration, systems engineering, and industrial engineering, as well as human and organizational behavior, which in turn contains large elements of psychology and sociology.

What Is Organizational Culture?

Organizations are made up of people, systems, and processes. The individual people who make up an organization are all unique in their own ways. So, too, are the systems in the organization, whether these systems are IT systems or otherwise. As well as processes connected to the systems and people, these processes are also unique to the particular organization.

This unique blend of people, systems, and processes defines an organization's culture. Certain types of organizations may well have similar kinds of cultures, however, they will not be exactly the same. For example, two different organizations in the same sector, such as insurance services selling the same kind of insurance services, would share similarities with each other but would not be identical. The always unique blend of people, systems, and processes makes the difference.

What Is Cultural Change?

When we talk about cultural change we are discussing the changes that need to occur in order to move from point A to point B within the organization. In the case of implementing an EDRMS solution we are fundamentally changing the way in which the people, systems, and processes work and relate to each other.

People

Change has to occur at the level of the individual. In the case of implementing EDRMS, the change that is required is a change of mindset in the way that individuals have been used to working. They have to be helped to make the change from using paper files and folders to using electronic documents and records and also using electronic documents and records with workflow, if this has also been integrated and implemented.

Systems

Implementing an EDRMS solution involves a significant change to the systems the organization uses for information, information in this case being documents and records. Here, we have one system, a manual system using paper files and folders stored in filing cabinets and filing rooms being replaced by its electronic equivalent of an EDRMS solution. The change that occurs within this system will have knock on effects of changes occurring with both the people and processes of the organization.

The system that is implemented needs to be able to provide advantages in terms of cost-saving, increased efficiency, and faster customer response in order to be justified as to replacing the old system. If the system can offer these advantages over the current system it is replacing, then this helps with the process of cultural change within the organization and helps the change process as a whole.

Processes

A number of the organization's processes connected with the storage and retrieval of information, information being documents and records will be significantly changed upon the implementation of EDRMS.

In the case of documents or records being placed in a file or folder, those documents and/or records will now be scanned, categorized, and indexed, then uploaded into the EDRMS document repository.

If workflow has been integrated with the EDRMS solution then documents and records will no longer be physically passed around the organization but will instead be electronically delivered to the users' work stations.

Workflow in itself represents a new process for people within the organization since documents and records will no longer be physically delivered but be electronically delivered. The post may also be electronically delivered to users' work queues via workflow; this too represents a significant change in the way that post is handled throughout the organization.

All these changes in processes require people to change their working methods, and the people aspect needs to be addressed by the change program.

Organizational Cultural and Change Management

Illustrated in Figure 18.1 is the link between the people, systems, and processes of organization culture and change management. The diagram displays the effect that changes to systems and processes have on people. This represents the massive cultural change that is taking place in both systems and processes. The representation of change management, at the bottom of the figure, that feeds into the organizational culture as represented by changing processes and systems shows what is required to help the organization cope with the cultural change.

Approaches to Change Management

As Change Management contains many other subjects, all of which are relevant to the process of change, there are as many approaches to it as there are practitioners. For example, some Change Management practitioners will use relevant aspects of NLP (neuro-linguistic programming), a branch of psychology, in their Change Program, whereas others will not.

As no two organizations are absolutely identical in the way they operate and function, this fact is also one of the most determining factors a particular Change Management practitioner will take in the approach to Change Management. It is very important to remember that organizations are made up of individual people, and since you are very unlikely to find two identical people, even in the case of twins, you will not find two organizations that are exactly the same — even if they were to use the same processes and systems.

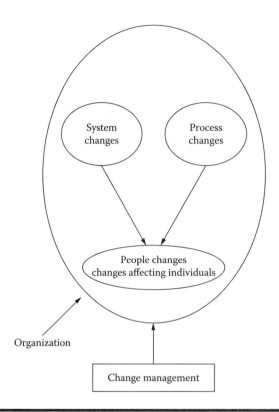

Figure 18.1   Changes to people, systems, and processes.

The process of Change Management and Managing Change within an organization requires many different skills, as well as a Change Management practitioner having an understanding of how subjects such as psychology, human and organizational behavior, and sociology play their role in the process of change. The change management practitioner will need to have political, analytical, people, system, and business skills.

Political Skills: Understanding Organizational Politics

Organizations are made up of people, hence groups of people make up social systems, therefore an organization can be considered a social system made up of different people all interacting with each other. Within these groups of people divided into different teams and departments there will be political issues. Certain types of organizations may be more political than others, but politics exists in every single organization and with all groups of people. The Change Management practitioner needs to understand how the politics in their organization works and the interaction throughout the organization.

Political issues within organizations can put up barriers of resistance to implementing new systems with some departments and teams resisting the implementation and other teams and departments actively encouraging and supporting the implementation. The Change Management practitioner must understand any particular issues, hidden agendas, and secondary gains that certain departments or teams may have regarding the implementation in order to know how to work with these departments or teams.

Analytical Skills: Investigating the Organization

A change management practitioner will need to be able to analyze specific requirements regarding the change program for different departments. An accurate and supported analysis of the needs and requirements of the organization as a whole as well as individual teams and departments within the organization will provide evidence and support the change management practitioner's findings in the requirements for the change program.

Detailed and accurate analysis skills are also required during the change program and once implementation of the system begins in order to evaluate progress of the implementation and report on the effect of the change program in a manner that reports are fully supported, using the correct analytical methods.

People Skills: Communication and Interaction

Organizations are made up of people, therefore the change management practitioner will need to have very good people skills and will need to know how to communicate with a variety of people from different departments and teams.

People skills include the ability to communicate with a variety of people to find out their specific needs and requirements regarding both the implementation of the new system and what impact the implementation of the new system will have upon their day-to-day working routines. The change management practitioner needs to gather this information and analyze it in order to develop the best method of change for those individuals, departments, and teams within the organization.

System Skills: Knowing the Organization Processes

The change management practitioner will need to get to know how an organization processes work, e.g., how do the processes within the sales team work and which processes do they employ for making sales, getting leads, following up leads, etc.

Business Skills: Knowing the Organization

The change management practitioner will need to know how businesses work and, in particular, how the business sector of the organization in which they are implementing the change program operates. This needs to cover information such as who are their customers, who are their suppliers, how does the organization generate income, who are the organization's competitors, etc.

Although there are significant differences between organizations in the public sector and not-for-profit sectors, the information mentioned above is still relevant, as all organizations have customers, suppliers, and the need to generate income, although with not-for-profit organizations the business drivers will be different. No matter which sector or industry the organization is in, the Change Management practitioner will still need to know how that particular organization/business works.

Fundamental Components of the Change Program

Although no two organizations are the same, there is an approach that can be followed step-by-step in designing a Change Management program. There are fundamental components of change programs that are applicable to the vast majority of organizations going through change.

Investigate the Culture of the Organization

The change management practitioner will need to come to grips with the culture of the particular organization where they are implementing the change program. The question has to be asked, how does the change management practitioner investigate the culture of the organization?

The answer is not as simple as listing a series of steps that the change management practitioner can follow in order to investigate the culture; however, spending time in the organization running workshops, interviewing teams and departments, and analyzing their working methods and defining their needs and requirements are some of the processes that can all help with the investigation into the company culture.

The Need for Change

The first step in formulating a change program is to justify the need for change. Here we need to ask "why" questions. In the case of implementing an EDRMS solution, the main "why" question is, "Why are we changing from using paper files and folders to EDRMS?" Making the formal case for EDRMS as well as creating a vision statement that is communicated to all staff can help in answering this question. If staff knows the reason for change and sees the benefits of change helping them in their day-to-day jobs, they will be more willing to embrace change, work with it, and accept it.

"The Computer Will Replace Our Jobs" Syndrome

Another question or assumption that staff may have, although they may not directly ask, is that the new computer system is being brought in to replace their jobs. This assumption commonly occurs where employees have been in their present jobs for a number of years, especially if the organization is also going through a restructuring process during the time that a new computer system such as EDRMS is being brought in. As part of the change program staff should be reassured that the new computer system is not going to replace their jobs, and their jobs are safe.

Communication with Staff

Adequate and effective communication with the staff of an organization is essential with any change program. So far, we have looked at the need to justify the need for change, as well the computer-will-replace-our-jobs syndrome. Now, let us image what could potentially happen if these issues are not adequately addressed: The organization's staff is not being told the reason for rolling out a new computer system, and the organization is also going through a restructuring program. Hence, you can understand why some staff may draw the conclusion, however incorrect, that the new computer system is going to replace their jobs.

Leading by Example

In order for a new computer system such as EDRMS to be accepted by the staff of an organization, those who are at the top of the organizational structure — directors and senior management — have to fully accept the system and the changes that the system will make to the organization, as this will help the majority of the staff within the organization also accept the system and the changes to working practices that come with the implementation of the system. Here, we are talking about leading by example.

Involve the Whole Organization

In the preceding section we have discussed the importance of leading by example. It is also important to involve the organization in the implementation of a new computer system such as EDRMS. Change starts at the top, gets driven by directors and senior managers, and then cascades down the layers through the organization, creating ownership of the new system and empowering staff at all levels.

Empowering Staff within the Organization

In creating ownership of the new computer system, in this case EDRMS, we are also empowering the staff within the organization, effectively giving them a part to play in the success or failure of the new system. This leads to a feeling of more authority and responsibility being handed to the average member of staff. Most would view this as a positive change, and it would have the effect of boosting morale, creating a positive buzz around the implementation of the new system.

Change at the Individual Level

It is important to realize that in order for change within an organization to be effective, that change must occur at the level of the individual staff member. In the case of implementing an EDRMS solution, it has been mentioned before that this represents a fundamentally new method of working.

In order for the system to succeed, staff members have to be willing to use the system and be willing to switch from paper files and folders to EDRMS. This change in mindset can be helped along by communicating the need for change, leading by example, involving the whole organization and empowering staff within the organization, which have been discussed in the preceding sections.

Expect the Unexpected

Change Management and the processes of change are not an exact science, and some would consider the Change Management area to be more of an art than a science. Any type of change can cause upheaval. Change and attempting to manage change can be a messy business with unexpected events occurring. It is important to have a flexible response towards unexpected events, as well as planning for the unexpected and running through different scenarios with different outcomes and different plans in place to counteract different outcomes. In essence, when any type of change is occurring, expect the unexpected.

Change Management Strategies

There are three well known change management strategies as described by Bennis, Benne, and Chin in their publication *The Planning of Change* (second edition; Holt, Rinehart and Winston, New York, 1969). These strategies are known as Empirical–Rational, Normative–Reeducative, and Power–Coercive.

Empirical–Rational

The Empirical–Rational Change Management strategy makes the assumption that change will occur within the organization because individuals are rational and follow their own self-interest, once that self-interest has been revealed to them. Successful change, therefore, occurs within the organization when the benefits of change are communicated to the individuals within the organization.

In order for the Empirical–Rational Change Management strategy to be effective, there have to be significant advantages with the proposed change, in this case, implementing an EDRMS solution to replace traditional paper files and folders. This strategy focuses on communicating the benefits of change, and the underlying theory is that communicating the benefits of change will win over staff within the organization. Therefore, they will adopt the new system favorably with enthusiasm.

Normative–Reeducative

The Normative–Reeducative Change Management strategy makes the assumption that people are social beings and want to fit in within the organization and the organization's culture — essentially be part of their organization.

This change management strategy focuses on redefining the way processes within the organization are performed and reeducating people to use those new processes. In the case of implementing an EDRMS solution, the emphasis here would be to introduce a new way of working, reeducating the staff of the organization, and helping to make the change. This change management strategy assumes that the organization's staff are compliant with the introduction and the new system, and that there is little resistance to the implementation of the new system.

Power–Coercive

The Power–Coercive Change Management strategy makes the assumption that people do what they are told to do, and that people are compliant with authority and orders given by an authority. This is a very authoritarian approach which essentially says "You will do as you are told, because you are paid to do so." In the case of the implementation of an EDRMS solution, the staff within the organization will simply have to use the new system because they have no choice in the matter.

Influencing Factors in Designing the Change Management Program

There are many influencing factors when designing the change management program. The primary factor is the individual culture of the organization. Other factors include the amount of resistance in the organization to new systems and new ways of working, the amount of time that the organization has to make the change and how quickly the system is going to be implemented, the average level of IT literacy within the organization, and the risk to the organization in terms of not implementing the system within a specific time period.

Which Change Management Strategy to Choose?

The decision regarding which change management strategy to choose depends upon the individual culture of the organization. However, in reality no one particular change management strategy on its own will be suitable, hence a hybrid approach is needed. Elements of all three change management strategies need to be incorporated into the change program for it to be successful.

A combination of the Power–Coercive and Empirical–Rational Change Management strategies tends to work best in organizations that are quite bureaucratic and where there may be high levels of resistance. Bureaucratic organizations tend to perform the same type of tasks on a regular basis, such as many public sector organizations do. Bureaucratic organizations also tend to have large numbers of staff who have been with the organization for a number of years and may well be set in their ways regarding how they perform their day-to-day tasks. The level of resistance here can be quite high when implementing new systems.

The Power–Coercive strategy aims to defeat the resistance within the organization by using the "iron hand" approach to change. The

Empirical–Rational strategy will also aim to reduce the amount of resistance within the organization by placing the emphasis on the benefits of change for the staff within the organization.

A combination of the Normative–Reeducative and Empirical–Rational change management strategies tend to work best in organizations that are more entrepreneurial, such as advertising or marketing agencies.

Using the Normative–Reeducative strategy, staff are gently encouraged to adopt the new system as a way of conforming to the organization, whereas the Empirical–Rational strategy places emphasis on the added benefits of adopting and using the new system.

However, as it has been said before, every single organization's culture differs, and therefore every single organization requires a slightly different approach to change and will require their own unique change management program. One size definitely does not fit all!

Overcoming the Reluctance to Let Go of Paper

A major factor of the change management program is encouraging staff to overcome their reluctance to not using paper. This issue may be extremely acute in cases where certain staff members have been with the organization for a number of years and are very set in their ways of carrying out their day-to-day tasks which may involve their keeping and filing their own paperwork.

The implementation of an organizationwide EDRMS solution means that they have to stop filing their own paperwork and instead either hand over paperwork to be filed by an administrative assistant or scan, classify, and index their electronic documents themselves. Although these particular people will probably comply with the EDRMS approach, they may still retain paper files and folders for their own use.

The change management program will need to address this issue by encouraging these users to give up their paper records and adopt the new electronic approach. Leading by example is one approach that can help to overcome this issue by line managers encouraging the new approach to EDRMS.

Changes in the Mail Room

If an organization has chosen to implement EDRMS within the mail room, using a method similar to the general letter module implemented using a workflow process, then this, too, is a big cultural change for the organization that needs to be addressed by the change program. Staff would have been used to receiving letters by hand and will be used to handling them in same way that they handle their domestic mail at home.

The new approach of receiving mail via a work queue in an electronic format will be loved by some and hated by others. The Change Management program also needs to address these specific changes by offering training and support to users who require this help.

Implementing and Managing the Change Program

Implementing and managing the change program is not going to be a simple task of do A, then B, and finally C. The change program will probably run over a fairly lengthy period of time such as two to three years, and change management practitioners responsible for implementing the program will need to be flexible in their approach, responding to the needs of the organization and incorporating these needs into the change program. A powerful ally in change can be others within the organization, staff that are willing to lead and help others with the change process. This then assists in creating a community of change within the organization and facilitates the change process in spreading throughout the organization.

For example, if the change program was devised and started off using one approach, and it became evident that this was not working, then the change management practitioner would need to modify their approach to the organizational change using other change methods that are more suitable.

Good change management requires the practitioner to break the rules at times, chucking out the rulebook and incorporating the "no rules" approach.

Conclusion

The subject of Change Management and all the related subject areas that accompany it is a massive area that this chapter cannot do justice to. The process of change is a complex one, which has to be tailored to each individual organization. The subject of change is an important factor when implementing any new system. Failure to adhere to the importance of change management and suitable change programs in implementing a new system such as EDRMS — or any new system, for that matter — could mean the system's failing or at the least not being able to reach its full potential within the organization. Adequate adherence to change management and the cultural change that occurs within organizations during the implementation of EDRMS is needed in order to make sure the system is successfully implemented and integrated into the organization.

Chapter 19

The On-Going Nature of the Project

It is important to realize that after the EDRMS solution has been implemented in the organization, including scanning historic paper documents and records, the EDRMS project does not stop and come to closure at this point. As technology moves on and new file formats come out with ever-increasing options for storing and retrieving images, so the EDRM system will need to keep abreast of these advances in technology by utilizing and incorporating suitable advances in technology into the EDRMS solution where appropriate.

The new EDRMS solution now lies at the heart of the organization as the system contains all the organization's information, documents, and records. Therefore, you will need to put mechanisms in place for receiving user feedback and supporting users. It is also advantageous to set up a working group that will meet on a regular basis to discuss advances in technology as well as user feedback and requests received, in order to determine how best to further improve the system in terms of usability and efficiency.

The EDRMS Working Group

Setting up an EDRMS working group is one of the methods that can be used to keep track of how the EDRMS implementation is progressing in terms of the solution meeting the organizational and users' needs and expectations, and generally how the solution has been received by the organization and the users within the organization.

The EDRMS working group should consist of the project sponsor and other members of the project board as well as the key user representatives that liaised with the project team while the solution was being implemented in their respective teams and departments. Other members of the working group can include legal representatives, IT support personnel connected with maintaining the EDRMS hardware, and administrative assistants who are involved with scanning and archiving documents and records.

Overall, the working group should consist of the key people involved with the EDRMS implementation. The EDRMS working group should meet on a periodic basis and put in place procedures and mechanisms for users within the organization to give feedback on the system in terms of requests and suggestions about the system and how to further improve it.

To keep the users on side after the implementation of EDRMS, user feedback should be treated seriously and not dismissed. No effort should be spared to make the users within the organization feel that they have their part to play in the system. Thus, we need to empower them within the organization. Encouraging user feedback can help to achieve this, as well as inviting users who have made suggestions to attend the EDRMS working group meetings and present their suggestions and feedback to the group.

Receiving User Feedback

The EDRMS working group can put in place several mechanisms to receive user feedback regarding the organization's implementation of EDRMS. The simplest and easiest method is to have an e-mail address link or a user feedback form placed on the EDRMS system pages.

A suggestion box is another option, and although this may be regarded as an outdated and old-fashioned method of collecting user feedback, it would provide the opportunity for those users who wish to remain anonymous or are concerned about using their desktop PC to give feedback regarding the system. The suggestion box gives the staff a chance to voice concerns anonymously.

Supporting Users

After the EDRMS solution has been implemented, it is very important to continue to fully support users in the use of the system, thereby encouraging them to explore the system and start using its more advanced features. Trainers who are themselves accustomed to the system and have been trained in its full use should be on hand to offer one-on-one training and group training sessions at short notice after the initial training in the system has taken place. The organization needs to actively support and encourage users by offering further training and top-up training to any user who requires or requests it.

In addition, members of the IT support team should be adequately trained in the use of the EDRMS to provide help and advice to staff in the use of the system. Key users within each department or team should also be able to provide help and advice.

Integrating the EDRMS with Other Systems

As mentioned at the beginning of this chapter, the EDRMS solution lies at the heart of the organization, with the document repository containing a very major proportion of the organization's information in the form of documents and records. Therefore, it makes sense to integrate the system with other systems within the organization. For example, a Customer Relationship Management (CRM) system that is concerned with the organization's customers can use the document repository and other features of the EDRM system to store documents and records relating to customer interactions.

Another example of a system that can be integrated with the EDRMS solution would be an Environmental Services system, which can also use the document repository of the EDRM system. In fact, any system within the organization that requires document storage can be interfaced with the EDRM system and can use its document repository.

The Paperless Office — a Myth or Practicality?

For over two decades the paperless office has been a point of debate. There is no doubt that EDRMS solutions significantly reduce the amount of paper within organizations, and using workflow to re-engineer business processes also cuts down significantly on the amount of paper traveling between departments within an organization.

Over the last decade or so, organizations in both the public and private sectors have made significant moves to reduce the amount of paper we need to use. For example, in the banking sector, many banks have introduced online-only personal accounts that do not send out paper statements. Citizens of certain countries are able to fill in and file their personal tax returns online, cutting out the step of both using and filing paper forms. There are many more examples of processes using electronic forms replacing paper forms.

Are we progressing towards having paperless offices? I would say we are. However, the change is not going to happen overnight; it will take a generation — or two. One of our major obstacles in achieving the paperless office or a paperless environment is our unwillingness to let go of paper! Hence, the question to ask is: Would you rather be reading this book in an electronic format on a computer screen or PDA (Personal Digital Assistant) device or be reading it as a book, leafing through the pages?

At this moment in time, our civilization is just so used to handling paper documents, paper records, paper books, newspapers, magazines, etc., that we do not want to get rid of paper. It is part of modern-day living. We already have the technology to go paperless; in fact, it's been around for a few years now. Who knows, maybe in ten years or so there will be even less paper in use than now, and then, in another ten years, even less than there was ten years prior to that. In a further decade down the line, paper may well have gone the way of the horse and cart, a symbol of our past. We'll just have to wait and see, since more efficient alternatives to habitual activities obviously aren't instantly and universally adopted.

Part 4

EDRMS CASE STUDIES

Case Study — Agis Healthcare, Netherlands

The healthcare market in the Netherlands underwent a significant change, moving from a private to a public model. This change put pressure on existing healthcare insurers to become more competitive with their pricing, quality, and service.

The insurer Agis Healthcare responded to this change by merging with three other regional healthcare providers to become more competitive. This resulted in Agis having a total of 1.2 million customers and over 2,000 staff, putting it in the top five largest healthcare insurers in the Netherlands.

Challenges

The Agis merger presented challenges to the company's documents and records procedures, as each newly united company was using different systems and had different filing procedures. This, in turn, made it very difficult to find information quickly, and when information needed to be located, it was a very laborious and time-consuming process.

Requirements

Agis wanted to reinforce their competitive position by both improving customer service while saving costs and implementing uniformity across their correspondence and recording systems.

Solution

Agis conducted a review of several products to help them accomplish their requirements. They settled on using StreamServe Financial. Agis uses StreamServe Financial in order to generate seven to eight million documents a year, including letters, invoices, policies, and settlement specifications from its mainframe system. The documents are laid out according to a corporate style template and then distributed as either letters, faxes, or e-mails depending upon the customer's preference.

Benefits

The benefits realized by Agis included increased efficiency of their correspondence processes, enabling them to help customers in a more efficient manner. Staff working in Agis' call center realized the immediate benefits of the application as all outgoing correspondence was stored in a customer's file, providing them with up-to-date information regarding a customer's situation at any time. The major benefit here for the call center staff is that they now have a digital folder that stores all the customer information, in one place, accessible from one central application.

Agis also realized cost savings of $200,000 in printing costs due to the uniformity of outgoing correspondence and the ability to report on the numbers of the outgoing correspondence, allowing the company to better manage its supplies.

Case Study — Barclays Bank, United Kingdom

Barclays Bank is one of the United Kingdom's leading financial institutions, offering both personal and business banking products and services to customers nationwide and employing over 75,000. Prior to 2001, the bank would process all employee-related records at its regional offices. Employee records were held in traditional hardcopy paper format, being stored in folders located in filing cabinets and filing rooms.

The Problem

The paper-based decentralized approach to human resources records was proving to be a very costly process with large amounts of information being duplicated across the company. In 2000, the bank decided to overhaul the decentralized HR service and to centralize HR services, addressing the issue of storage as well as how to utilize technology to provide a solution. After investigating various options regarding the issue of storing the employee files, the option that made most sense to the bank was to scan the employee files and store them as images in an electronic system.

The Solution

Barclays Bank implemented a solution from Open Text along with optical storage technology for the document management requirements of their HR function, allowing them to capture over 75,000 employee files, storing them in a central repository while providing secure electronic access to authorized users, and, as a result, was able to eliminate a massive amount of paper documents and folders. This resulted in significant savings for the bank in connection with monthly storage costs, as well as reduced costs and savings regarding document retrieval.

The Benefits

With regards to the money saved on storage costs, Barclays estimated that they would have needed 250 sq m of storage space, costing about £14 per meter — around £3,500 per month. As well as the storage costs, the bank would have needed to employ at least ten people to maintain the storage facility that would have cost at least another £10,000 per month.

Additionally, the implementation of EDRMS has provided a secure centralized electronic system that is able to help Barclays maintain legal compliance regarding data protection and other acts of law and regulations while also significantly reducing the risk of data loss through IT back-up and disaster recovery procedures. Currently, the EDRMS solution holds approximately 12 million images, comprising 75,000 employee records and 220,000 pension files.

Barclays has also managed to reduce the amount of manpower required for their HR function quite dramatically. By centralizing the HR function and at the same time implementing EDRMS, the bank has managed to reduce the HR workforce from 1700 personnel to 900 personnel.

The HR section currently receives up to 600 benefit forms per day, which amount to around 3000 pages. However, Barclays only needs to employ one person to scan and index these forms into the system.

Barclays has been able to maximize office space by removing filing cabinets now that all employee files are electronically held, resulting in every employee being able to have a window view in the office. This has subsequently led to a more open, collaborative environment, resulting in greater teamwork between colleagues.

Due to the increased productivity and costs saved due to the implementation of EDRMS, Barclays has decided to build upon this by implementing an internal call center for employees, using Siebel Customer Relationship Management (CRM) software. The bank has also integrated the EDRMS solution with the CRM solution, effectively creating a link to employee records and files held within the two and enabling call center staff to retrieve employee records located within them. All related e-mails and incoming and outgoing correspondence are stored within the EDRMS system. With the addition of Siebel Workflow software, requests can be forwarded to the relevant HR person for action.

By combining EDRMS, CRM, and Workflow software, Barclays have managed to significantly reduce costs in all areas and significantly increase productivity across the HR function, leading to reduced complaints from its employees. This has resulted in much greater improved internal customer service to its employees.

Case Study — City of Newark, New Jersey

The City of Newark, New Jersey, was required as per the mayor's mandate to leverage technology to streamline business processes and improve collaboration. Thus, an aggressive plan was adopted to achieve a paperless administration, because managing the vast amount of paper documents the city departments created was becoming increasingly inefficient, with documents being misplaced and unnecessarily recreated.

Solution

The City of Newark implemented Xerox DocuShare, which provided rich content handling, collaboration, and workflow, and was implemented together with the scanning, imaging, and printing hardware technology needed to permit the move to a paperless environment by allowing incoming mail and paper documents to be scanned into the system and electronically sent around the City of Newark's departments.

After customizing the user interface of Xerox Docushare, the City of Newark branded and launched its new document management and digital imaging system as Newark Document Express (NDEX).

Benefits

The implementation of Xerox Docushare along with a Xerox production printer, 50 Xerox desktop scanners, and 25 Xerox multifunction devices allowed the City of Newark to realize the benefits of paperless administration, digital print management, federal E-File compliance, and the benefits of delivering municipal council meeting agendas electronically.

Paperless Administration

Paper documents of all types, including all incoming mail, is scanned and indexed into the system so that the documents can be electronically routed throughout the organization using workflow.

Digital Print Management

All jobs for the City of Newark's print department are created, stored, and approved within DocuShare. Print jobs are then sent directly from DocuShare to the Xerox production printer.

Federal E-File Compliance

All court filings, orders, and rulings are scanned into the system for transfer to the federal courts in compliance with the federal courts e-filing requirements. This has allowed the City of Newark to reduce its paper file storage and increase communication, allowing attorneys and staff to communicate more efficiently and effectively.

Municipal Council Meeting Agendas

Prior to installing the system, an average of 100 agendas had to be printed and mailed out to the constituents of town hall meetings. With the implementation of the system, the agendas are stored as PDFs, and a URL is sent to the attendees so they are able to download the agenda, saving staff time, paper, and postage costs.

Further Improvements

Following the successful implementation of Xerox DocuShare, the City of Newark plans to further utilize the solution in the areas of workflow, digital forms processing, and collaborative services, as well as integrating DocuShare with PeopleSoft for electronic handling and storage of human resources content.

A public extranet will be developed to distribute commonly requested information and forms to the public and private constituents via DocuShare. The extranet will help to improve the City of Newark's response time for requests to public records by making this information available via the extranet. Online forms submission will also be developed by integrating DocuShare with Verity's LiquidOffice.

Case Study — Cuatrecasas, Spain

Cuatrecasas is one of the largest independent law firms in Spain and Portugal. The company has over 600 attorneys spread across 17 cities throughout Spain and Portugal, with further offices in Brussels, New York, and Sao Paulo. The company specializes in all areas of business law covering finance, tax, litigation, and labor laws. It advises more than a fifth of the Spanish Fortune 500 companies and more than half of the top 35 Spanish listed companies.

Being one of the most prestigious law firms in Spain, the company needed to constantly improve collaboration and information exchange among employees located in different offices. The company did not have an information management strategy that incorporated the whole organization, and this led to a number of limitations, presenting the following challenges.

Exchanging Information

Due to each individual office having its own filing system, lawyers within the company did not have any way to search for or retrieve information stored throughout the organization. If staff needed information from different offices, lawyers and other staff needed to send e-mails requesting the information, resulting in delayed waiting times.

Document Version Control

E-mail was the only way for lawyers and staff to exchange documents across company offices, and this led to version control issues, i.e., differences between the same documents. The differences soon started to appear, resulting in different versions of the same document located at different offices.

The lack of document version control was severely obstructing the company's goal of standardizing their information assets, documents, and records.

Publishing Company Information

The company used an intranet to publish information such as internal announcements and company documents for lawyers and staff within the organization. However, this had become a cumbersome process with bottlenecks building up as IT administrators had to post the content. This severely limited the amount of content that could be published on an ongoing basis.

Low Reuse of Best Practices

Because of the company's existing infrastructure, it was not possible to create online collaborative groups that shared common interests around certain aspects of business law, or that were centered around geographical areas, and other similar categories that facilitated best practices for lawyers.

The Requirements

The organization needed to implement a solution that provided document management and record management functionality that was able to provide for the document and sharing needs of lawyers and other staff, regardless of which office they were based in.

The system also needed to provide access to documents and information via a Web client and to support the publication of Web-based content.

The Solution

In early 2001, the company started to evaluate products from a variety of vendors and, after the selection process, chose Hummingbird's Enterprise solution in December 2001 as it offered a broad range of functionality out of the box and was also able to be customized on an ongoing basis as dictated by the needs of the organization.

From April 2002 to June 2002 the IT department at Cuatrecasas set up the product, defining user profiles and standardizing taxonomies. In June 2002, the implementation phase began, and the company started a full-scale deployment of the system, initially rolling out the solution to their Madrid and Barcelona offices and completing it in October 2002. Cuatrecasas then began rolling out the solution to its remaining offices worldwide in November 2002. User Training began with the rollout of the solution to the Madrid and Barcelona offices and was completed for all employees by the middle of January 2003, by which time almost 1000 employees had been trained in the use of Hummingbird Enterprise.

The Benefits

By implementing both document management and collaborative services across the organization, the company standardized information sharing across its offices worldwide. The company has achieved the following benefits:

Increased Productivity

The ability for all employees, especially attorneys, their secretaries, and other administrative assistants to quickly and easily search, retrieve, and share information globally, regardless of location, has meant that best-practice content can now be reused easily. It is estimated that there has been a ten percent reduction in the time formerly spent on document management prior to the implementation of Hummingbird.

Publishing

With the implementation of Hummingbird Enterprise, Cuatrecasas is now able to publish nearly three times the content it could previously. Content is also published three to four times faster. In order to publish this level of content without Hummingbird, the company would have had to employ a full-time IT employee at an annual cost of $50,000 per year.

Infrastructure

By implementing a single, centralized document management system (DMS) across the whole of the organization, Cuatrecasas has been able to reuse and redeploy file servers used for individual office's separate file systems. In addition to reusing and redeploying file servers, Cuatrecasas has also been able to save costs for file servers for the five new offices that the organization expected to open over the following three years.

Increased IT Productivity

Prior to the implementation of a single, centralized document management system across the whole of the organization, IT personnel spent almost ten percent of their time maintaining separate file systems and its associated infrastructure at individual offices. Now that Hummingbird Enterprise has been deployed throughout the organization, the maintenance time for information assets has been significantly reduced, as maintenance only needs to be performed on a single document management system.

Client Extranet

The company has also developed and deployed a client extranet that allows clients to log on and retrieve key documents via the Web without the need to contact attorneys' administrative staff. This has led to increased efficiency for both attorneys of the firm as well as their administrative staff and has also improved client care.

Costs

The main costs of the project over a three-year period included software, consulting, personnel, training, and hardware. The software costs, at 42 percent, represented the single largest cost and included the cost of Hummingbird licences and annual maintenance fees. The consulting costs in the initial year accounted for 25 percent of the total spent, whereas the time spent by Cuatrecasas IT personnel on the initial deployment and ongoing system support accounted for 15 percent. Upgrading Cuatrecasas' storage area networks and servers accounted for 7 percent of the costs. The remaining 11 percent of the costs was spent on items such as training users and miscellaneous expenses such as travel.

Calculating Return on Investment (ROI)

The total cost of the implementation included software, hardware, consulting, personnel, training, and other investments, and was calculated by Nucleus Research Inc., in order to quantify Cuatrecasas' total investment in Hummingbird Enterprise.

The annual ROI was 84 percent, and the project was able to pay for itself in just over one year. Direct benefits attributable to the implementation of Hummingbird Enterprise were savings in infrastructure costs, as the organization was able to redeploy equipment such as file servers that were previously used for disparate file systems located in separate offices.

As the implementation of the Hummingbird portal offered much quicker and easier publishing processes, the organization was also able to save approximately $50,000 per year by not needing to employ a full-time IT person to publish content on the Web site.

The indirect benefits achieved through the implementation of Hummingbird Enterprise included the increased productivity of all staff located in dispersed geographical locations as a result of the organization no longer needing to maintain separate document and record systems.

Time is also being saved for users of the system as they are able to search for and retrieve documents much faster. IT staff are spending less time maintaining and supporting multiple systems. Cuatrecasas also expects to make savings to administrative time and resources, once the client extranet has been fully rolled out.

Case Study — NHS Care Records Service, United Kingdom

The National Health Service (NHS) Care Records Service is probably the largest implementation of EDRMS anywhere in the United Kingdom, if not globally, at the present moment. In the United Kingdom, the majority of healthcare is provided publicly by the state, and the NHS is one of the largest public sector organizations, comprising all public hospitals, doctor's surgeries, health centers, and other health-related organizations.

The NHS Connecting for Health program, a program sponsored by the U.K. government, is responsible for the implementation of the NHS Care Records Service, which is expected to be completed by 2010.

Under the NHS Care Records Service, every patient, which amounts every citizen in the United Kingdom, will have an NHS Care Record that has two parts — a Detailed Care Record and a Summary Care Record. The detailed care record will consist of full and detailed notes of the patient's record, whereas the summary care record will be built up from the information held in the detailed care record and contain essential information such as allergies the patient has and medications the patient is currently receiving. In total, over 50 million patient records will be contained within the NHS Care Records Service — a record for every citizen in the United Kingdom.

Access controls to patient records are determined by the role of the healthcare professional who is caring for the patient. For example, a receptionist working at the hospital may only be able to view information such as the patient's name, their doctor's name, and the condition they are being treated for, without being able to change the record, whereas the patient's doctor may have full access to their patients' records and will be able to update them to reflect the care a patient is receiving.

By 2008, it is planned for all citizens to have access to their electronic care records, accessible via a secure and protected NHS Web service known as HealthSpace. It will allow patients to add information regarding their needs and preferences such as wheelchair access and organ donation.

There are also a number of other electronic initiatives under way that are being implemented in parallel with the NHS Care Records Service. These are Choose and Book, Electronic Transmission of Prescriptions (ETP), Picture Archiving and Communications Systems (PACS), and Quality Management and Analysis System (QMAS).

Choose and Book

Choose and Book is an electronic booking service that allows patients requiring referrals to a specialist the choice of up to four different hospitals and clinics. The system also allows patients to book hospital appointments on a date and at a time and location that suits them.

Electronic Transmission of Prescriptions (ETP)

ETP is an electronic prescription service that will allow doctors to electronically send their patients prescriptions to pharmacies. Patients are able to nominate the pharmacy they collect their prescriptions from and not make a visit to the doctor's surgery in order to get a repeat prescription.

Picture Archiving and Communications Systems (PACS)

The PACS system is an electronic imaging system used for the storage and retrieval of patients' x-rays and scans, allowing for faster diagnosis than if the images were printed on film, and filed and distributed by hand.

Quality Management and Analysis System (QMAS)

The Quality Management and Analysis System allows patients to provide feedback to doctors and hospitals on the type and level of care they received.

Primary Care Trusts

The NHS is made up of Primary Care Trusts (PCTs), which cover different regions of the United Kingdom. Each PCT has been given the authority to select its own service provider for the implementation of electronic patient records.

Case Study — Nevada County, California

In 1999, all of Nevada County's departments, 28 in total, were using different systems for organizing, storing, and retrieving information. Some departments were planning to restructure and improve their systems, but there was a lack of a coordinated overall approach to storing information. The Information Systems Department of Nevada County realized this and identified the need for the implementation of a single information system to contain all of the County's internal and public information.

Xerox DocuShare, together with the Xerox FlowPort scanning system used with a Xerox Document Centre digital multifunction device, was selected by the Information Systems department to solve the County's document management problems.

The County also undertook a major project to expand the online information and interactive services available to the public and especially residents of Nevada County. This happened around the same time as the County procured Xerox Docushare. A series of vehicle emission reduction grants from the Northern Sierra Air Quality Management District also allowed the development of a government Web site so that citizens and businesses could interact with the County without having to drive to County buildings. The County's Web site utilizes the Affino Content Management System developed by Emojo, a U.K.-based company.

Both the document management project and Web content management project came together as a result of every County document being stored in "DocuShare Collections." As each DocuSahre Collection or file is given a Web-based URL, this made it extremely easy for the County to allow the public access to public information in the forms of documents via the County's Web site.

Implementing document management through DocuShare encouraged collaborative working between staff in the same department and across departments. Having easy access to documents via the Web encouraged a cultural change within the organization and encouraged staff to share information and work cooperatively on projects.

An additional benefit of implementing document management in connection with the content management system employed on their Web site meant that the County was able to reduce the amount of car trips made to county buildings.

Through extensive Web site tracking and ongoing surveying of facility visitors made between October 1, 2000, and April 30, 2002, overall trips to the county buildings in order to get forms or information were significantly reduced, equating to a saving of 65,000 round trips during the period. Hence, the implementation of a document management solution at Nevada County has helped reduce auto emissions, and it is also environment friendly.

Case Study — New York City Police Pension Fund, New York

The New York City Police Pension Fund (NYCPPF) provides retirement, disability and pension, and loan benefit services to over 75,000 members, both active and retired police officers. When the NYCPPF split from and became a separate entity from the New York Police Department (NYPD), the organization decided to reevaluate its current systems and technology.

Part of NYCPPF's charter was to encourage and foster an environment focusing on teamwork and customer service. Thus, the organization wanted to help its employees, 130 in total, to access and share information by creating an internal online portal.

The Challenges

The organization also had to overcome the inefficiencies associated with relying on manual paper processes that were making it incur costs in terms of staff time and storage. There was a 15-year microfilm backlog of members' personnel documents stored in over 75,000 folders located in filing cabinets in a filing room. Each time an employee needed a file, he or she would need to travel to the filing room and search through the cabinets to attempt to locate the file. On occasion, however, upon searching through the cabinets, the employee would realize that the file was already with another employee. Employees would then return to their desks empty handed and send out e-mails asking if anybody had the particular file they were looking for. This would mean that it could take the staff as many as several hours to locate a single file.

Another challenge the organization faced was the amount of time and money they were using to print up information for their executive meetings. Each month the 12-member board of trustees met to review issues such as disability cases. This required the organization to print up 15 packets of information, with each packet containing 15,000 pages or more. This was costing the organization over $10,000 per year on paper alone, apart from the costs associated with employee time and equipment costs for printing and copying.

The Requirements

NYCPPF was using quite significant resources, both with the storage and retrieval of members' personnel files as well for printing costs for the executive board meetings. A solution was required that would help the organization cut down on unnecessary paper and associated costs and allow them to store and retrieve documents using less resources in terms of staff time and storage space.

The Solution

The first solution explored by NYCPPF was using microfilm to transfer the documents contained in the 75,000 personnel files. The organization quickly realized that this would take several years to complete, and therefore ruled it out.

The organization started looking at document management solutions, and as NYCPPF was already using Xerox multifunction products, they decided to implement Xerox DocuShare. Scanning America was commissioned to convert the organization's personnel folders into PDF format. The files were scanned and stored in Windows NT directories named after the personnel folder members' identification numbers, and then moved into DocuShare using the drag-and-drop functionality found in the DocuShare Windows Explorer client. This has resulted in all the personnel folders being stored online within DocuShare and now allows documents to be searched for quickly and easily, allowing employees to retrieve them within minutes if not seconds. Compared to the previous situation of staff members having to physically locate files in filing rooms, the conversion of the members' personnel folders has saved the organization's employees massive amounts of time.

Besides saving the organization time, converting the documents into an electronic format has allowed the NYCPPF to implement a disaster recovery solution. All documents stored within the DocuShare repository are backed up to tape nightly and archived at a secure offsite location, allowing for the quick restoration of documents in case of service interruptions. As well as nightly backups on to tape, NYCPPF has also implemented data replication software, using NSI DoubleTake, which automatically replicates content uploaded in DocuShare to an offsite disaster recovery site.

Due to the confidential nature of the documents handled by the organization, all scanning had to be carried out and completed on site. Once the documents were scanned into the DocuShare, security access permissions were set up to allow only authorized employees access to the files.

NYCPPF uses seven Xerox Document Center scanning devices for its daily imaging needs, which involves the scanning of hardcopy documents and the subsequent conversion of these documents into PDF format, allowing them to be uploaded into DocuShare and retrieved by users within the organization using the DocuShare Web client. NYCPPF currently scans in up to 800 documents per day as part of its daily business process.

Besides using document management to create an online central repository for members' personnel files, the organization is also using the DocuShare system for other document- and forms-based business processes, including retrieving and filling in human resources forms, reviewing and studying computer-based training materials, and creating and posting executive board of trustees documents and calendar items.

The Benefits

NYCPPF has achieved a good ROI upon the implementation of document management and has been able to implement the solution without requiring additional IT staff. The organization currently employs ten IT members of staff, of which just two need to perform part-time maintenance tasks on the system. In essence, NYCPPF has been able to make significant moves towards "the paperless office" while working with a limited budget.

The implementation of document management at NYCPPF, through implementing Xerox DocuShare, has provided benefits in a number of key areas. These are listed here:

All 75,000 member personnel files have been converted into electronic documents, and are held as PDFs within DocuShare. The 75,000 member personnel files, hold a total of around 110,000 documents that represent about 10 million individual pieces of paper. This would have taken about 15 years to transfer to microfilm, however the documents were converted to their current electronic form in 6 months.

The implementation of document management has meant that NYCPPF has been able to implement a disaster recovery plan. Prior to the implementation of document management, the organization only had one hardcopy of each document, so, in the event of a disaster, these documents would have been irretrievably lost. Now, with document management, in the unfortunate event of a disaster, the documents would be able to be recovered from the secure offsite disaster recovery site.

Prior to the implementation of document management, NYCPPF was producing 15 packets of documents for the executive board meetings, with each packet being around 15,000 pages in length. Storing the documents in DocuShare has saved the organization over $10,000 in paper costs alone, not counting the cost of associated staff, and printing and copying costs. The documents are now copied onto two CDs, with the IT staff providing these and laptops to board members, thereby saving costs and allowing board members to review the documents quickly instead of having to wade through extremely large bundles of paper.

Increased employee efficiency, teamwork, and collaboration have been achieved by implementing document management.

The implementation of a Web-based document management system has led to the implementation of an information portal that gives employees quick and easy access to information such as computer-based training, data held in Oracle databases, human resources forms and policies, and team Web sites. The information portal also allows users to manage collaborative spaces such as bulletin boards, project folders, and project/team calendars.

The solution has also led to more effective communication within the organization. The HR department uses the document management system for the induction of new employees and keeping current employees informed by storing forms and company announcements within the system.

Case Study — Trinity Community Centre, United Kingdom

The Trinity Community Centre (Trinity) is a charity-based organization in the United Kingdom that runs a number of schemes aimed at helping immigrants in settling into their local areas and helping them to build a new life.

The organization helps immigrants, referred to as members, of all ages, origins, and genders. It offers advice and support to approximately 16,000 members each month, helping them with regard to their own individual circumstances.

Trinity runs various projects such as "Childcare and Youth," "Educational," "Creative and Cultural," and "Project DOST." Project DOST provides long-term specialist and individual support for asylum-seeking children who have arrived in the United Kingdom as unaccompanied minors. The organization believes that it is every child's right to receive a good education, along with healthcare and housing. It is committed to helping these children receive their full statutory entitlements. Project DOST, which is an Europewide project, offers these children a holistic educational and creative program, offering a safe and secure place for them to grow by improving their self-esteem and self-confidence and allowing them to develop friendships.

The project was established in 2002 and has grown from a single project with two part-time staff working with just 15 children to one that now employs five full-time, one part-time, and five freelance staff, supporting over 150 children per year.

The Issues

Trinity was handling large amounts of paper-based records and correspondence, which were all filed in filing cabinets. This system was proving more and more difficult to maintain as time went on, and paper documents would sometimes be filed incorrectly. Another issue facing the organization was that of security and confidentiality. Due to the sensitive nature of the information held and the manual filing process, a structured security scheme was difficult to implement, maintain, and govern.

Frequently, freehand notes and interactions with members such as telephone conversations were not attached to the members' files, leading to vital information being overlooked and resulting in a duplication of work efforts.

As a charity-based organization, for Trinity to gain funding for the next financial year, it has to prove that it is effective in serving the community; hence, submitting end-of-year reports on members' progress and reports based on certain groups of members was becoming increasingly difficult. Thus, success stories were overlooked, leading to a negative impact on Trinity's funding for the following year, ultimately reducing the number of members Trinity was able to help.

The Solution

In order to combat the decreasing efficiency of the organization, Trinity commissioned the services of One Degree Consulting, a U.K.-based consultancy specializing in document and records management solutions, to investigate the issues that Trinity was experiencing and then to undertake a feasibility study to ascertain whether an EDRMS solution would solve the organization's issues, and also to ascertain if an EDRMS solution was both financially and physically viable. The feasibility study concluded that Trinity required a full EDRMS solution with the ability to add notes and other interactions to members' records by the organization's staff.

To meet the requirements of Trinity highlighted in the feasibility study, One Degree Consulting recommended an EDRMS solution called workFile. The workFile product suite is an EDRMS solution developed by One Degree Consulting, which contains a number of modules, all which could be quickly and easily customized and delivered within Trinity's budget.

The functional specification was developed and a modeled solution was created within workFile. A bespoke interface was also created to allow quick and easy building of reports specific to Trinity and their funding requirements. Business rules specific to Trinity were also incorporated into the solution using the workFile business operations layer.

The workFile content module allowed electronic documents to be stored, retrieved, and securely managed, and allowed the organization to capture a variety of documents including faxes, scanned documents, e-mail, and audio and video files. The workFile records module was also configured in order to provide the record management functionality required by Trinity.

The workFile CRM core module was implemented as well and is being used to manage interactions with members and record notes in an electronic format against members' records. The CRM module also allows the organization to record all staff interactions with members' records and provides full auditing capability, allowing the organization to ascertain which staff member has accessed which records, the actions they performed, and when they accessed the record.

The complete solution, consisting of the content, records, and CRM modules was implemented by One Degree Consulting on time and within budget and has not only met Trinity's needs but exceeded its expectation. The solution has allowed the organization to save both space, in the context of storage of members' records, and time, in the context of the previously manual handling and management of records. It has allowed Trinity to concentrate more resources towards their core business — helping its members.

Case Study — Tyler Memorial Hospital, Tunkhannock, Pennsylvania

Tyler Memorial Hospital serves more than 50,000 patients per year and, as the only hospital in the county of Tunkhannock, provides a range of diagnostic and therapeutic services.

Challenges

The effective treatment of patients requires both doctors and nurses to have fast access to the most recent medical charts of the patients, which were retrieved by staff members in Tyler's medical records department from the hospital's storage room. When the records department was closed, nursing supervisors had to take up the task of retrieving medical records, which meant they had to delay their primary duty of providing care to their patients. Locating documents in the 200-sq ft storage room was becoming increasingly difficult and time consuming.

State regulations stipulated that all medical records were to be completed within 30 days and then stored for a period of at least seven years after their completion. Medical charts would pile up, as the hospital did not have an efficient method of identifying the charts that could be destroyed from the charts that still needed to be retained in order to satisfy the state regulations. Reports regarding individual patients also needed to be sent to relevant physicians for their patients' continued treatment. To avoid the hospital becoming liable if it was not able to prove that physicians did receive the reports, the records staff faxed the reports using RightFax, saving every fax-delivered electronic notice. To provide a legal backup for the hospital, files were transferred to Microsoft Word and saved as documents each day. Additionally, an extra post was created and departmental hours were increased to free up nursing staff from the tasks of locating patient records.

Solution

Tyler Memorial Hospital commissioned Comprehensive Microfilming and Scanning Services, a local vendor, to help them automate the record management processes for their Health Information Management Systems (HIMS) using Captaris Alchemy Document Management. The implementation of EDRMS allowed the hospital to connect different departments within the hospital allowing for quick and efficient access to records in order to both update records and retrieve them from a variety of different locations.

The hospital now archives all records, lab results, and other documentation using the Alchemy solution, which allows this information to be electronically available to all authorized personnel. Nurses are able to retrieve records right at their station, and doctors are able to dictate discharge summaries from any location within the hospital.

The integration of RightFax and Alchemy allows staff to send and receive electronic faxes from their desktops and easily store them within the Alchemy solution. This has significantly decreased the hospital's risk of liability with regard to doctors not receiving reports because all faxes can now be easily searched for and retrieved.

Results

By implementing the Alchemy document management solution integrated with RightFax electronic fax software, the hospital has been able to improve its documentation service to both hospital staff and doctors, resulting in improved patient care. The solution has also helped the hospital to meet its obligations in complying with state regulations regarding the retention of patient records. The solution has also resulted in the hospital saving the costs associated with employing a member of staff in a full-time position to maintain records, the cost of which amounts to at least $22,000.

The implementation of the document management solution has also allowed authorized personnel to access medical records from home offices through an intranet, increasing efficiency and resulting in faster revenue turnaround. Future plans are in place to allow doctors from outside the hospital site access to medical records from their own offices in a secure fashion. This has also helped the hospital to comply with state regulations, which stipulate 30-day completion times for medical records. The Records Management module of Alchemy also alerts administrative staff when records have reached the legal time limit for being retained, thus allowing them to easily and quickly dispose of records.

Converting paper files into electronic images has meant the hospital has been able to reduce the amount of storage space needed to house files. This has enabled Tyler Memorial Hospital to save both costs and space associated with the storage of files and reduce the amount of man hours needed to maintain paper-based filing.

Appendix A

EDRMS Software Vendors*

Diagonal Solutions — Wisdom

Diagonal Solutions provides a component-based approach to ECM called Wisdom. The components consist of Document Management, Record Management, Rendition Services, Imaging, Collaboration, Workflow, Content Management, and Commerce. By offering a component-based solution organizations can implement those modules that they require and also add on to an existing installation at a future date.

The Wisdom Document Repository is the core product that underpins all the other modules. The Document Repository provides a secure managed repository for each information asset deposited into the system.

Wisdom's Document Management component provides document management functionality that includes version control and auditing of documents as well as allowing security to be defined using a multi-tier security model.

The Records Management component allows an organization to retain and manage records both in paper and electronic formats. Wisdom Imaging offers document capture functionality, allowing historic paper-based documents to be scanned in using OCR (Optical Character Recognition) for type and ICR (Intelligent Character Recognition) for handwriting, and storing within the Document Repository.

---

* By including a short summary of vendor's products, the author is by no means endorsing any one particular product over any other. Furthermore the author highly recommends that readers who need to procure a software solution carry out their own independent research.

Wisdom Workflow allows an organization to create business process workflows enabling documents to be routed around the organization between staff and departments.

Further information on Diagonal Solutions Wisdom offering can be found online at http://www.diagonal-solutions.co.uk.

Dexmar — KnowPro EDRM

Dexmar offer a solution called KnowPro. KnowPro is available as a combined EDRM system, called KnowPro EDRM, that incorporates Document Management, Records Management and Customer Relationship Management functionality, or as separate document and records management modules known as KnowPro Document Management and KnowPro Records Management, respectively.

Functionality is provided around facilities to enable scanning incoming documents and routing them around the organization. Electronic documents can be produced based on corporate standard templates and stored in the system. E-mail management is catered for, allowing incoming and outing e-mails to be placed within a central repository for future access. Document life cycles can be created to facilitate records management allowing documents to be classified as records and then disposed of using rules-based criteria defined by the organization. Security features allow file (document) level security settings to be set on documents. Notifications can be set up that alert users to changes and activities around certain documents or sets of documents within the organization.

IBM Lotus Domino technology underlies KnowPro products. The Records Management module can be implemented with other IBM Domino document management systems including IBM Domino Document Manager (formerly Domino.Doc).

Further information on KnowPro can be found online at http://www.dexmar.com.

EMC Software — Documentum Records Manager

EMC Software offers a Records Management solution called Documentum Records Manager, which is one of a range of products on offer from EMC. Functionality in the Documentum Records Manager includes file plan administration, classification, compound records, Microsoft Outlook integration, automated capture, records disposal, and digital shredding of records among other functionality.

Documentum Archiving Servicing for Imaging is one of the products offered by EMC Software to provide document and record archiving functionality, allowing historic paper-based documents and records to be scanned and stored as electronic images.

Documentum Content Management Portlets offers both document management and workflow functionality, allowing users to store and retrieve many different types of content. Organizations are able to set up and define cabinets, which in turn contain folders, where documents and content would be stored. The workflow functionality allows an organization to create and define workflow processes allowing items in a workflow list to have certain actions taken on them such as forwarding, rejecting, or dismissing.

Further information on Documentum Records Manager can be found online at http://software.emc.com.

Fabasoft — eGov-Suite

Fabasoft has developed a product called eGov-Suite that has been designed to match European Public Sector requirements as well as offering country-specific modules. The eGov-Suite is a comprehensive package aimed at public sector organizations and specifically provides document management, records management, and workflow features. In addition to providing EDRMS functionality, the Fabasoft eGov-Suite also targets the areas of Online-Official Business, Content Management, Knowledge Management, e-Business, New Public Management, and Employee Self Service and Citizen Relationship Management.

Document management functionality includes imaging capabilities, allowing an organization to scan in historic paper documents and store them electronically within the system. Version control and release levels of documents are provided as well.

Records management functionality allows an organization to set up and maintain the storage records, specifying how long they need to be retained and how and when they need to be disposed of.

Activity Management allows for work-based processes such as orders, quotes, invoices, and proposals to be based around business process workflows, allowing these documents to be forwarded and routed around the organization. Fabasoft's eGov-Suite also provides SAP R/3 integration. Further information on Fabasoft's eGov-Suite can be found online at http://www.fabasoft.com/.

FileNet

FileNet has developed a range of products that can be used to implement an EDRMS solution. Among the products are FileNet Content Manger, FileNet Records Manager, and FileNet Business Process Manager. FileNet Content Manager provides document management functionality along with workflow functionality. Further information on FileNet's products can be found online at http://www.filenet.com.

Hummingbird — DM, RM, R/KYV

Hummingbird has developed a range of document and records management products called Hummingbird Enterprise. The products relevant to EDRMS are Enterprise DM, Enterprise E-mail Management, Enterprise R/KYV (R/KYV is pronounced "archive"), Enterprise RM, and Enterprise Workflow.

Hummingbird Enterprise DM provides document management functionality using a single repository to store and retrieve documents. Hummingbird Enterprise E-mail Management captures and stores corporate e-mail and can be integrated with major e-mail systems such as Microsoft Outlook, Novell Groupwise, and Lotus Notes. Enterprise RM provides records management functionality, allowing physical and electronic records to be managed and audited and disposed of according to legislative rules. Enterprise Workflow allows organizations to set up and define business process workflows, allowing documents to be routed around the organization as the documents' activity progresses.

Hummingbird Enterprise R/KYV is an EDRMS solution aimed at government departments, and includes document, records, and e-mail management as well as workflow. Further information on Hummingbird's product offerings can be found at http://www.hummingbird.com.

Hyperwave — eRecords Suite

Hyperwave offers an EDRM solution called eRecords Suite that is aimed primarily at public sector organizations both in the United States and United Kingdom. As well as providing records management functionality, eRecords Suite also provides document and content management, collaboration, and business process support.

The Records Management functionality of eRecords Suite consists of Classification Scheme Management to classify records and documents using folders and metadata, Search and Retrieval, Retention and Disposal, and Access Rights Management, allowing security settings to be applied to records and documents, and contains auditing and reporting features as well.

eRecords Suite is a module of Hyperwave's eKnowledge Infrastructure, and can be used on its own or with other applications from the eKnowledge Infrastructure. Further information on Hyperwave eRecords Suite can be found at http://www.hyperwave.com.

IDOX — Document Management and Records Management

IDOX offer a modular approach to EDRMS, offering separate document management, records management and workflow software. The records management module effectively sits on top of the document management module.

The Document Management software consists of five components: scan, index, browse, image viewer, and DDE Integration. The components — scan, index, browse, and image viewer — are connected with converting paper documents and records into their electronic format, indexing them and retrieving them on screen. The DDE Integration module allows the organization to integrate the Document Management software with an existing back office system, thereby providing a document repository to other systems.

The Records Management module sits on top of the Document Management module and consists of three components: browse, records administrator, and image viewer. The records management module consists of the following features: classification schemes, folders, reports, retention and disposal, and security and administration functions allowing administrators of the records management system to set up and modify the records management functions. Further information on IDOX Document Management and Records Management software can be found at http://www.idoxplc.com.

Meridio

Meridio offer several products for EDRMS solutions that integrate with Microsoft Office and Microsoft's Sharepoint Portal Server.

The Meridio Office System integrates with Microsoft Office providing document and records management functionality to the Microsoft Office Suite of programs. Meridio for Microsoft SharePoint Portal Server provides plug-in records management functionality for Microsoft SharePoint Portal Server.

The Meridio suite of programs uses Microsoft's SQL Server as the repository for the document metadata database. Meridio E-mail Archiving integrates with Microsoft Outlook to provide functionality for the storage and archival of e-mail. Further information on Merido's EDRMS solutions can be found at http://www.meridio.com.

IBM

IBM's EDRMS solution consists of DB2 Document Manager and DB2 Records Manager. DB2 Document Manager's functionality includes compound document support, rules-based document lifecycle management, desktop application integration, and support for engineering file formats, version control, and automated notifications, among other features.

DB2 Records Manager is a records management engine that can manage a variety of documents as records. It is used in conjunction with DB2 Document Manager and DB2 Content Manager. DB2 Content Manager is available in three different packages, with different document and records management capabilities. The DB2 Content Manager Basic Complete Enterprise Offering includes document management and workflow capabilities. The Complete Enterprise Offering of DB2 Content Manager includes Lotus® Domino.Doc®, WebSphere®, MQ Workflow, DB2 Content Manager, DB2 CM OnDemand, DB2 CommonStore, DB2 Records Manager and DB2 Document Manager.

The Complete Enterprise offering is a complete EDRMS solution. The DB2 Enterprise Edition contains all the functionality of the DB2 Content Manager, Complete Enterprise Offering as well as additional Web services and XML functionality. Further information on IBM's Document and Records Management solutions can be found at http://www.ibm.com.

Interwoven

Interwoven offers several products for document and records management solutions. The records management solution is called RecordsManager, and integrates with Worksite, Interwoven's document management solution. Interwoven's RecordsManager is aimed at professional services firms such as law and accounting.

Worksite is offered in the following versions. Worksite MP is a collaborative document management solution that combines document management functionality together with collaboration software functionality. Worksite MP Records Management Server integrates with Worksite MP to extend the collaborative document management functionality with records management. Other modules available for Worksite MP include an Adobe PDF Server module, MS Office integration, MS Outlook integration, and Lotus Notes integration.

WorkRoute MP is Interwoven's workflow offering that integrates with Worksite MP enabling workflow and automated business process to be created and set up. Further information on Interwoven's Worksite and RecordsManager can be found at http://www.interwoven.com.

Objective

Objective offers a modular approach to electronic and document management. Modules on offer include Electronic Document Management, Records Management, Drawing Management, Web Content Management, Workflow, Application Integration and Infrastructure Integration.

The Objective Foundation module provides the system infrastructure for all other modules and needs to be implemented before any other module. The Foundation module's functionality includes the user interface, security settings, audit trails, metadata definition, user management, and searching facilities. By implementing a combination of Objective's Foundation module, Electronic Document Management module and Records Management module, you will have implemented an EDRM system.

Objectives Application Integration module provides an SDK (Software Development Kit) that provides programmers with access to the functionality of Objective components allowing for customization or bespoke development in-house. Objectives Infrastructure Integration provides a range of Xlink modules that allow you to provide integration between Objective's modules and the organization's applications.

Further information on Objective's document and records management solutions can be found online at http://www.objective.com.

Open Text Corporation

Open Text Corporation offer a range of documents and records management products known as the LiveLink ECM product range. Document Management software is offered in three different versions: LiveLink ECM — Document Management is a general-purpose document management solution that provides full lifecycle management for any type of electronic document; LiveLink ECM — Production Document Management is aimed at high-volume and the secure long-term archiving of electronic documents that would be needed in the financial services and utilities industry; and LiveLink ECM — Production Imaging is mainly aimed at organizations that need to scan and archive historical paper documents.

Records Management software also comes in a variety of different versions catering for different organizations. LiveLink ECM — Records Management provides a general-purpose implementation for Records Management and connects to other LiveLink ECM systems such Document Management. LiveLink ECM — Regulated Documents is aimed at pharmaceutical, financial, utility, and government organizations that are subject to regulations regarding the modification of electronic documents. E-mail archiving and storage is catered for with LiveLink ECM — E-mail Management products.

Further information on Open Text Corporation's range of document and record management solutions can be found at http://www.opentext.com.

Tower Software

Tower Software's solution is called TRIM Context Enterprise Content Management. The TRIM Context platform includes the Electronic Document Management, Records Management, and Workflow, E-mail Management, Reporting, Document Assembly, Collaboration, Imaging, Integration, and Web Content Management modules.

Electronic Records Management functionality found in TRIM Context consists of Record Classification, Record Security, Retention Management, Archival and Disposal Management, and Physical Tracking of Records.

The Document Assembly module integrates with Microsoft Word and allows for documents such as contracts and legal papers to be automatically assembled using standard clauses and contact information in the document repository.

E-Mail Management allows e-mails to be captured from most popular e-mail platforms, enabling users to catalogue e-mails and link e-mails folders to folders within the TRIM Context repository. The Imaging module consists of functionality to allow documents to be scanned into the document repository as well as offering OCR (Optical Character Recognition) features to allow for document context searching and retrieval of documents. Further information on Tower software's document and records management solutions can be found online at http://www.towersoft.com.

Uniplex

Uniplex offer a range of products and solution for document management and workflow called onGo. Their main products are onGo DMS Server for document management and onGo Workflow Server for business process management, as well as onGo Portal that provides an application framework in terms of a SDK (Software Development Kit). These products are known as the onGo server technologies.

Modules that integrate and extend the onGO server technologies are available and include onGo onWEB, a Web-client; onGo WindowsClient, a Microsoft Windows-based client; onGo onDAV, a Windows Explorer client; and onGo MS-ADDins, which allows direct access from Microsoft applications to onGO DMS. onGO MAILocate enables e-mail functionality, onGO inMotion enables offline working, onGO DocRouter enables knowledge management, and onGO onSearch offers sophisticated search mechanisms.

Uniplex also offer a range of industry and department DMS solutions. onValid provides management of QA (Quality Assurance) documents. onStaff provides online recruitment and electronic personnel documents. onContract provides electronic contract management. onGovernment is aimed at public administration and provides both workflow, document management and archiving facilities. onCare provides information management for health insurance companies, and onPublic provides information management for chambers and councils.

Further information on Uniplex's document management and workflow solutions can be found online at http://www.uniplex.com.

Vignette

Records & Documents is Vignette's EDRMS offering that incorporates functionality such as Records Management, Electronic Information Capture, Imaging and Indexing, e-mail archiving, and collaborative document services.

Records & Documents uses a single repository to store all documents and records within the system. Imaging and Indexing facilities allow the organization to scan and index paper-based documents and store them within the systems repository. E-mail facilities allow for the capture of both internal and external e-mail and instant messages for long-term storage, retrieval, and auditing.

Collaborative document services allow users in the organization to manage documents created from application suites such as Microsoft Office. Documents can be stored in the systems repository and retrieved. Document check-in and check-out functionality is included as well versioning, auditing, and document review. Vignette offer document and records management aimed at specific business solutions and industries. Solutions on offer include Collaborative Document and Records Management solutions and Imaging and Workflow solutions. Further information on Vignettes Records & Documents can be found online at http://www.vignette.com.

World Software Corporation

World Software Corporation has developed a product called WORLDOX GX, a document management system that is aimed at legal and financial services organizations.

The functionality of WORLDOX includes document management and e-mail management capabilities, as well as collaboration features. Document management features include document check-in and check-out, version control, work lists, integrated file viewing, file activity auditing, reporting, file-level security, and more. WORLDOX integrates with both the Microsoft and Corel Office Suites, as well with ODMA (Open Document Management API) compliant scanning software.

The e-mail management functionality allows WORLDOX to be integrated with Microsoft Outlook, GroupWise, and Lotus Notes, allowing e-mails to be stored and retrieved from the document store. The software can also be set up to automatically store e-mails based on certain criteria and rules.

WORLDOX software is built around a dual database architecture, which uses distributed databases, as well as a central database, that has the added benefit of providing resilience. For example, if the central database were to become unavailable, then documents could still be retrieved from a distributed database. On the other hand, if one of the distributed databases were to go down, then information could still be retrieved from the central database.

Further information on WORLDOX GX can be found online at http://www.worldox.com.

Xerox DocuShare

Xerox Corporation produce a family of document and records management products known as Xerox Docushare, which are the Xerox DocuShare Enterprise Content Manager, Xerox Docushare CPX Enterprise Content and Process Manager, and Xerox Docushare Records Manager.

Xerox Docushare Enterprise Content Manager offers document and content management functionality including document routing and approval, check-in and check-out of documents, version control, and collaboration and publishing facilities. Docushare Records Manager can be integrated with this product to offer a full EDRMS solution.

Docushare CPX Enterprise Content and Process Manager has added workflow and business process management functionality that can provide support for repetitive document processes such as invoices and forms. The product includes the use of a dashboard that supports work queuing and process participation, meaning invoices and forms can be routed around the organization. Docushare Records Manager provides full Electronic Records Management functionality allowing an organization to define and work within compliance policies and procedures in classifying and declaring records.

Further information on the Xerox Docushare family of products can be found online at http://docushare.xerox.com/.

Appendix B

Glossary

AS 4390-1996 Australia's Record Management standard released in 1996, developed by the IT/21 Committee of Standards Australia, in conjunction many other private and public sector organizations in Australia. The standard was released in February 1996 but has since been superseded by ASO 15489.

AS ISO 15489 The latest Australian standard on records management published on March 13, 2002 replacing the AS 4390-1996 standard on records management in Australia.

Auditing With regards to both electronic documents and electronic records, auditing refers to recording the actions performed upon an electronic file, whether that file be an electronic document or electronic record or any other form of electronic content.

Business Process Management (BPM) Refers to the management of an organization's activities, known as processes that are carried out in the organization. For example, a retail bank has a process for opening a new account.

Business Process Re-engineering (BPR) Refers to the improvements that can be made to an organization's processes in terms of making the process more efficient to the organization. For example, a retail bank would analyze their new account opening process and then by using Business Process Re-engineering methods see how the organization can improve the efficiency of the process.

Business Case A document that justifies the implementation of a new system in an organization. The business case will often include long-term savings, cost of implementation, and benefits to the organization.

Business Analyst A Business Analyst is a person responsible for analyzing the needs of an organization and then recommending and proposing solutions. With regards to EDRMS, a business analyst would first investigate how the organization is currently storing documents and records and then recommend solutions for electronic systems.

Change Management Change Management refers to the methods used within an organization to manage the change that occurs whenever new systems and processes are introduced.

Change Program A Change Program is the collection of change management methods and practices that an organization uses in order to effect change.

Check-In Refers to the state of a document when it is placed within the document repository and is available for users to access.

Check-out Refers to the state of a document when it has been copied out of the document repository and is available for the user who checked out the document to make changes to the checked out document before checking in the document with those changes.

Collaboration Refers to the sharing of content, such as documents, Web pages, or any other type of content used by persons within an organization or across organizations.

Content Management Refers to the management of all different types of content including creating new content, editing content, and deleting content. Enterprise Content Management systems manage many different types of content including documents, records, and Web pages among others, while Web Content Management Systems manage purely Web-based content.

Classification Refers to classifying documents or records according to a pre-determined document type, such as Invoices, Orders, Health and Safety, etc.

Cultural Change Refers to the changes that an organization goes through when new systems or processes are introduced.

Customer Relationship Management (CRM) Computer systems that manage the relationship between organizations and their customers.

Data Protection Act The Data Protection Act is an English act of law that is concerned with how organizations store personal information about individuals.

Designing and Implementing Record Keeping Systems (DIRKS) An eight step methodology developed by the Archives Authority of New South Wales, Australia. The DIRKS methodology is included in ISO 15489 International standard and the Australian standard AS ISO 15489.

Document Image Processing (DIP) Document Image Processing refers to computer systems that are able to store and process images. DIP systems generally refer to older image processing systems that pre-date many modern electronic document and records management systems.

Document Repository The document repository refers to the electronic database that stores all content for an electronic document and records management system.

Document Types Refers to the different classification of documents and records according to which type of document they are, e.g. Invoices, Orders, etc.

DoD (Department of Defense) 5015.2-STD "Design Criteria Standards for Electronic Records Management Software Applications" A standard developed by the U.S. Department of Defense for the design of Electronic Records Management Systems. This is the de facto standard used in the United States.

Document Management (DM) Refers to the management of documents. Most commonly, the term Document Management is used to refer to an electronic document management system.

Document Management System (DMS) Refers to a system that is used to manage documents. As with the term DM the term DMS most commonly refers to electronic systems that manage documents.

Enterprise Content Management (ECM) Enterprise Content Management refers to computer systems that are able to handle all types of content within an organization such as documents, records, Web content, and many other forms of content.

Electronic Document Management (EDM) Refers to systems that are able to electronically manage documents.

Electronic Document Management Systems (EDMS) Refers to systems that are able to electronically manage documents. Essentially the same acronym and term as EDM.

Electronic Document and Records Management (EDRM) Refers to systems that are able to electronically manage documents and records.

Electronic Document and Records Management System (EDRMS) Refers to systems that are able to electronically manage documents and records. Essentially the same acronym and term as EDRM.

Electronic Document Types Refers to the different classification of electronic documents and records according to which type of document they are, e.g. Invoices, Orders, etc.

Electronic Records Keeping (ERK) Refers to the electronic system used to store and manage records.

Electronic Records Keeping Systems (ERKS)   Refers to the electronic system used to store and manage records. Essentially the same acronym and term as ERK.

Electronic Records Management (ERM)   Refers to electronic systems that are used for the electronic management of records.

Electronic Records Management System (ERMS)   Refers to electronic systems that are used for the electronic management of records.

E-mail Management   Refers to systems that manage and store e-mails.

Freedom of Information (FOI)   Freedom of Information is concerned with acts of law, which exist in most developed countries around the world, which govern the rules organizations must follow in satisfying requests for information from individuals and other organizations concerning information that the organization holds, e.g., a customer of a retail bank can put in a Freedom of Information Request to receive a copy of the information the retail bank holds on them.

Freedom of Information Act (FOIA)   The Act of Law that contains the rules and regulations regarding Freedom of Information requests in a particular country.

Folder Structure   Refers to a hierarchical structure that contains layers of folders.

Functional Requirements   Functional Requirements define the functions that a computer system needs to perform in order to meet the organization's needs.

Indexing   Refers to systematically categorizing documents, records, and other content according to the type of content.

International Organization for Standardization (ISO)   An international organization that produces standards specifications for almost any kind of system, process, or procedure.

ISO 15489   An international standard that defines best practices for the management of both paper and electronic documents and records produced by the International Organization for Standardization (ISO).

Metadata   Refers to the values that are held against documents, records, and other types of content in order to index and categorize the content in a systematic fashion.

Model Requirements for the Management of Electronic Records (MOREQ)   MOREQ is a European standard for electronic records management that was developed by the IDABC (Interoperable Delivery of European eGovernment Services to public Administrations, Businesses and Citizens). MOREQ, also referred to as Model Requirements, is a functional specification of the requirements for the management of electronic records. It is a functional specification that can be applied to both the public and private sectors as well electronic and manual (paper-based) records management systems.

Neuro-Linguistic Programming (NLP)   A branch of psychology that is sometimes incorporated into change management programs to help facilitate the process of change within the organization.

Optical Character Recognition (OCR)   Computer software that is able to recognize typed text on paper documents which are then scanned in and converted to electronic formats.

Open Document Model Architecture (ODMA)   An open interface that is used by Microsoft® Office based applications to allow other programs to communicate with them.

Project Management Body of Knowledge (PMBOK)   A collection of processes and knowledge that provides guidance on best practice within project management produced by the Project Management Institute.

Project Initiation Document (PID)   A document that is produced by the PRINCE2™ methodology which includes the plan and cost of the project as well as providing justification that a viable Business Case exists for the project.

Project Manager   The person who is responsible for projects and who manages the day-to-day activities of the project.

PRINCE2™   PRINCE2™ stands for **PR**ojects **IN** Controlled **E**nvironments and is a project management methodology developed in the United Kingdom by the Office of Government Commerce.

The Privacy Act   The Privacy Act of 1974 is a U.S. Act of Law that is concerned with how information relating to citizens is stored and the rights that citizens have regarding access to the information stored about themselves.

Records Management (RM)   Refers to the management of both manual and electronic records.

Retention   A Records Management term that describes the action of retaining a record for a specific period of time. Most commonly records are retained within an EDRMS.

Remote Access   Refers to accessing a computer system from a remote location away from where the main computer system and its networks are based.

Repository   A central store that can contain any type of data and information in the form of computer files, such as documents, records, graphics, sound recording, movie clips, etc.

Search and Retrieval   A term used to describe the functions needed to find document, records, and other content that are stored within a computer system.

Technical Requirements   Refers to the technical design and requirements of a system. The Technical Requirements are normally compiled into a document.

TNA 2002 A definition of functional requirements for Electronic Document and Records Management Systems developed by The National Archives of the United Kingdom. In order for software to be TNA 2002 compliant, records management software vendors must design their software according to the rules laid out in the TNA 2002 Functional Requirements.

Version Control Version Control is the method of tracking changes made to documents and content. Normally Version Control tracks document changes using version numbers.

Web Content Management A computerized system that manages Web content and Web sites allowing content to be created, edited, and deleted as needed.

Workflow Workflow, which is also referred to as business process management (BPM), is used to manage the flow of information around an organization.

References

Bielawski, L. and Boyle, J., *Electronic Document Management Systems*, Prentice Hall, NJ, 1997.

Jenkins, T., *Enterprise Content Management*, 3rd ed., Open Text Corporation, Ontario, Canada, 2005.

Glazer, D., Jenkins, T., and Schaper, H., *Enterprise Content Management Technology*, 4th ed., Open Text Corporation, Ontario, Canada, 2005.

Jenkins, T., Kohler, W., and Shackleton, J., *Enterprise Content Management Methods*, Open Text Corporation, Ontario, Canada, 2005.

Managing Information and Documents: The Definitive Guide, 17th ed., Cimtech, 2006.

Chapter 3 — Legislation and Standards

Bailey, M., ISO 15489: A Practical Guide, http://www.egovmonitor.com/node/1401, 2005.

Australian Government — National Archives of Australia, The DIRKS Manual, http://www.naa.gov.au/recordkeeping/dirks/dirksman/contents.html, 2003.

U.S. Department of Defense, DoD 5015.2-STD, Design Criteria Standard for Electronic Records Management Software Applications, http://www.dtic.mil/whs/directives/corres/html/50152std.htm, 2002.

IDABC, MOREQ: Model Requirements for the Management of Electronic Records, http://ec.europa.eu/idabc/en/document/2631/5585, 2001.

The National Archives, Functional Requirements for Electronic Records Management Systems, [TNA 2002], http://www.nationalarchives.gov.uk/electronicrecords/reqs2002/, 2002.

The National Archives Approved Electronic Records Management Systems — Top 10 Questions, http://www.egovmonitor.com/node/181, 2005.

InfoUSA, Selected Laws — http://usinfo.state.gov/usa/infousa/laws/majorlaw.htm.

The Privacy Act of 1974, 5 U.S.C § 552a — http://www.usdoj.gov/oip/privstat.htm, 2003.

BSI PD 0008 — Document Management Legal Admissibility, http://www.falcon-documentmanagement.co.uk/legal/bsipd0008.html, 2006.

Chapter 11 — Scanning Historical Documents and Records

25,000 Warrington PCT Paper Patient Records Converted in 14 Days, http://www.elision.com/casestudies/index.php?article_id=15.

Chapter 12 — Project Management

Office of Government Commerce, Managing Successful Projects with PRINCE2, 2002.

Project Management Institute, A Guide to the Project Management Body of Knowledge, 1996.

Chapter 18 — Managing the Cultural Change of EDRMS

Nickols, F., Change Management 101 — A Primer, http://home.att.net/~nickols/change.htm, 2004.

Nauheimer, H., The Change Management Toolbook, http://www.change-management-toolbook.com/home/introduction.html, 2005.

Dooley, J., Cultural Aspects of Systematic Change Management, http://www.well.com/user/dooley/culture.pdf.

Booz Allen Hamilton, Ten Guiding Principles of Change Management, http://www.boozallen.com/media/file/138137.pdf, 2004.

Bennis, W.G., Benne, K.D., and Chin, R. (Eds.), *The Planning of Change* (2nd ed.), Holt, Rinehart and Winston, New York, 1969.

Case Studies

Agis Zorgversekeringen, KnowledgeStorm.com, http://www.knowledgestorm.com.

Barclays Bank — Streamlining HR Processes, OpenText Corporation, http://www.opentext.com.

City Government Goes Paperless — KnowledgeStorm.com, http://www.knowledgestorm.com.

ROI Case Study: Cuatrecasas — Hummingbird, http://www.hummingbird.com.

NHS Connecting for Health — Health care records.

Nevada County Citizen's Integrated Information Portal — KnowledgeStorm.com, http://www.knowledgestorm.com.

New York City Police Pension Fund (NYCPPF) — 2005 ComputerWorld Honors, http://www.cwhonors.org.

A Case Study of the Trinity workFile Implementation — One Degree Consulting Ltd., http://www.consulting-onedegree.com/downloads/articles/Trinity Case Study.pdf.

Tyler Memorial Hospital Speeds Delivery of Patient Records with Captaris — Captaris Customer Case Study, KnowledgeStorm, http://www.knowledgestorm.com.

EDRMS Software

Diagonal Solutions — Wisdom, http://www.diagonal-solutions.co.uk.

Dexmar — KnowPro EDRM, http://www.dexmar.com.

EMC Software — http://software.emc.com.

Fabasoft — eGov-Suite, http://www.fabasoft.com/.

FileNet, http://www.filenet.com.

Hummingbird — DM, RM, R/KYV, http://www.hummingbird.com.

Hyperwave — eRecords Suite, http://www.hyperwave.com.

IDOX — Document Management and Records Management, http://www.idoxplc.com.

Meridio, http://www.meridio.com.

IBM — http://www.ibm.com.

Interwoven — http://www.interwoven.com.

Objective — http://www.objective.com.

Open Text Corporation — http://www.opentext.com.

Tower Software — http://www.towersoft.com.

Uniplex — http://www.uniplex.com.

Vignette — http://www.vignette.com.

World Software Corporation — http://www.worldox.com.

Xerox Docushare — http://docushare.xerox.com/.

Index